RAF Airman Selection Test: Training Manual.
Guide with Practice
& Skills Test Published on Amazon
© 2022

Introduction

Congratulations on taking your first step in deciding to join the Royal Air Force. The aptitude test is the most critical part of the process as it will determine which military occupational specialty you are best suited to. This guide is designed to help you prepare for the RAF AST through a three-step approach. First, this book will describe what the AST is and how it affects your career. Secondly, we will break down each section of the exam to give you a detailed description of the layout with tips and tricks to help get you through the section. Finally, you can practice on 300 sample questions to help familiarize yourself with the format. Note: the practice problems are based on the actual test but are not the exact questions you will see.

About the AST

The AST is administered at your nearest Armed Forces Careers Office and is designed to test an individual's aptitude and skills to determine which careers they are best suited to. It is a multiple-choice with five possible answers.

The test consists of seven sections:

1. Verbal Reasoning
   a.   20 Questions
         15 Minutes
2. Numerical Reasoning
   a.   Part I   12 Questions
       4 Minutes
   b.   Part II   15 Questions
       11 Minutes
3. Work Rate
   a.   20 Questions
         4 Minutes
4. Spatial Reasoning
   a.   Part I   10 Questions
       4 Minutes
   b.   Part II   10 Questions
       3 Minutes
5. Electrical Comprehension
   a.   22 Questions
         15 Minutes
6. Mechanical Comprehension

	a.		19 Questions
		13 Minutes	
7.	Memory		
	a.	Part I	10 Questions
	b.	Part II	10 Questions

The score you earn directly correlates to the number of military occupational specialties available to you as most require a minimum score. It is in your best interest to score as high as possible. Unanswered questions are counted against you.   You do not have a time limit for these practice exercises; your objective is to identify the patterns and answer as many questions correctly as possible. With continued practice, you will naturally pick up speed.

Verbal Reasoning

The verbal reasoning section tests your English comprehension skills and ability to interpret and reason what you have read. You are given a passage to read, followed by a series of questions relating to that passage.

Numerical Reasoning

Numerical reasoning contains two parts. Part I consists of basic math involving addition, subtraction, multiplication, and division. Part II tests your ability to interrupt numerical information.   You will not be allowed to use a calculator, although you will be given scratch paper.

Work Rate

Work Rate is a series of codes consisting of numbers, letters, and shapes. Your task is to identify a matching code. This section has the largest question to time ratio, so you'll need to work quickly and accurately.

Spatial Reasoning

Spatial reasoning consists of two parts. Part I assess your 2D ability in fitting objects together. Your task is to visualize what a series of shapes would look like when put together. Part II involves 3D shapes that are shown from various perspectives. Your task is to pick the original shapes after the perspective changes.

Electrical & Mechanical Comprehension

The electrical and mechanical comprehension portion covers topics taught in GCSE-level physics and covers a wide range of material. If you have trouble with some of the problems in this book, I highly recommend taking time to review some GCSE material in-depth on your own as a refresher.

Memory

The memory section consists of two parts. In Part I, you will be shown a series of sequences/patterns that you will be asked questions about. In Part II, you will be shown grids that have squares that have been colored in. Your job will be to memorize the pattern and then correctly identify the pattern you were just shown if the patterns were put together. Unlike the previous portions of the test where you will be working from a test booklet, this last portion of the test will be presented to you on film.

Test Tips

- Read the questions and answers carefully; eliminate as many options as possible.
- Don't leave blank answers. Blank answers and wrong answers are treated the same, do not leave any questions blank.
- If you do not know an answer, try working backward from the possible options before guessing.
- You may not need to solve the entire question to choose the correct answer. For example, we know the last digit of 0.345234+0.234521 will be a 5. Therefore, we are looking for an answer that ends with a 5.
- If you have extra time after answering all questions, review your answers. It's easy to misread a question or make a mistake.
- Know your multiplication tables
- Don't try to cheat
- There are NO trick questions.
- Keep practicing – it will help prepare you for the real test.
- Don't practice with a calculator. You will not be able to use a calculator on the actual test.
- Use the test to take the test. That means use the multiple-choice options you are given to help you answer or answer the question more quickly, as the answer is one of those four options.
- Be mindful of your time, but work quickly and accurately.

The Day Before
- Eat healthy and try to get a good night's sleep.
- Familiarize yourself with how to get to the test location with the expected travel time. Don't forget to take into account traffic or unexpected delays.

On Test Day
- Eat breakfast (or, if you prefer, a smoothie) and do some brief physical activity.
- Avoid drinking too much water or coffee so that you do not have to use the bathroom during the test.
- Arrive early to the test location with time to spare so that you do not feel rushed and have time to adjust to the surroundings.
- Relax, you know the format of the test and the types of questions that will be asked. YOU'VE PRACTICED!
- HAVE CONFIDENCE IN YOURSELF!!

Verbal Reasoning

You will be shown a short passage and asked four questions relating to the paragraph you just read. Choose the best answer for each of the questions.

Text #1

Steve and Tim are brothers. Tim golfs every weekend unless it is raining, in which case he will go to the cinema. On Saturdays, Steve likes to run, and on Sunday, he goes bowling with John and Harry. If it is the first week of the month, then Charles will join in bowling. Tim golfs on Saturday with John and Charles but goes to the cinema with Clyde. Clyde and Harry are also brothers.

1. If it's raining on Saturday, what is Tim doing, and who is with him?
    A. Golfing with John and Harry
    B. At the cinema with Clyde
    C. At the cinema with John and Harry
    D. Golfing with John and Charles
    E. At the cinema with Charles

2. It is the first Sunday of the month and Tim is golfing. What is Steve doing and who is with him?
    A. Running with John and Harry
    B. Bowling with John, Harry, and Charles
    C. Running with Tim
    D. Running with John, Harry, and Clyde
    E. Bowling with John and Harry

3. There are two sets of brothers. What are their names?
    A. Steve & Tim and Clyde & Harry
    B. John & Harry and Steve & Tim
    C. Steve & Harry and Charles & John
    D. Charles & Steve and Clyde & Tim
    E. Larry & Tim and Hector & Charles

4. Who runs by themselves?
    A. Clyde
    B. Harry
    C. Steve
    D. Tim
    E. John

Text #2

Five ships set sail from London.
> Ship A travels to New York
> Ship B travels to Cape Town
> Ship C travels to Bahrain
> Ship D travels to Mumbai
> Ship E travels to Hong Kong

The ship traveling to North America is carrying cars and is the longest in length. The ship going to Hong Kong carries chemicals, and the ship going to Mumbai contains medicine. The ship going to Bahrain is bringing textiles but makes a stop in Egypt. The ship carrying chemicals is the fastest but has the furthest journey. The ship going to Cape Town is the shortest in length. The ships traveling to Hong Kong and Mumbai are longer in length than Ship B, but both are shorter than the ship going to Bahrain.

5. Which ship is the fastest?
     A. Ship A
     B. Ship B
     C. Ship C
     D. Ship D
     E. Ship E

6. For which ship do we not know its cargo?
     A. Ship A
     B. Ship B
     C. Ship C
     D. Ship D
     E. Ship E

7. What is the second longest ship?
     A. Ship A
     B. Ship B
     C. Ship C
     D. Ship D
     E. Ship E

8. Which ship stops in Egypt?
     A. Ship A
     B. Ship B
     C. Ship C
     D. Ship D
     E. Ship E

Text #3

Five employees make reservations at the same hotel. Each employee stays on a different floor. Steve stays on the lowest floor possible. Jonah is twice as high up as Sara. Doug has to climb two floors to get to the gym. The hotel is 20 stories tall. There are no rooms on the first floor. Sara is staying 6 floors above Steve. Jonah has the highest room of all employees. Ashley's floor is below Sara's. The gym is six stories from the top of the hotel.

9. What floor is Sara on?
   A. Floor 4
   B. Floor 5
   C. Floor 6
   D. Floor 7
   E. Floor 8

10. Who is on the 20th floor?
    A. Jonah
    B. Sara
    C. Tim
    D. No one
    E. Steve

11. Who is on the second lowest floor?
    A. Ashley
    B. Sarah
    C. Steve
    D. Doug
    E. Jonah

12. What floor is Doug on?
    A. Floor 12
    B. Floor 13
    C. Floor 14
    D. Floor 15
    E. Floor 16

Text #4

A factory produces vehicles according to the following schedule

	Sunday	Monday	Tuesday	Wednesday	Thursday	Friday	Saturday
Week 1		Red 4 door sedans	Red 4 door sedans	Green vans	Green vans	National Holiday off	Green vans
Week 2		Blue trucks	Closed for maintenance	Closed for maintenance	Blue pickup trucks	White 2 door sedans	White 2 door sedans
Week 3		Company day off	Blue SUVs	Red SUVs	White SUVs	White trucks	White trucks
Week 4		White trucks	Blue trucks	Blue 4 door sedans	Blue Vans	Company day off	Closed for maintenance

13. Toby works Monday through Friday. If he works every day available, how many days did he work during the four weeks shown?
    A. 14
    B. 15
    C. 16
    D. 17
    E. 18

14. Vehicles leave the facility every Saturday by rail. If the shipment contains, Vans, Sedans, and trucks, what week of the month is it?
    A. Week 1
    B. Week 2
    C. Week 3
    D. Week 4
    E. None of the above

15. Sara never works at the factory when trucks are produced. Which day of the week does she work?
    A. Monday
    B. Wednesday
    C. Thursday
    D. Friday
    E. Saturday

16. Adriene joined the company during the month shown. She only worked on 4 door sedans, vans and trucks. Which day of the week was her first day?
    A. Tuesday
    B. Wednesday
    C. Thursday
    D. Friday
    E. Saturday

Text #5

Amy's dog is bigger than Jerome's but smaller than Kory's. Derrick and Lily have the same size dog and the same color of fur. Lily's dog is larger than Jerome's but smaller than Amy's.

17. Who has the largest dog?
    A. Amy
    B. Jerome
    C. Kory
    D. Derrick
    E. Lily

18. If smaller dogs are smarter than larger dogs. Who has the smartest dog?
    A. Amy
    B. Jerome
    C. Kory
    D. Derrick
    E. Lily

19. Derrick's dog has brown fur. What color is Lily's dog?
    A. Brown
    B. Black
    C. White
    D. Stripped
    E. Spotted

20. If Derrick and Amy switch dogs. Who has the second largest dog?
    A. Amy
    B. Jerome
    C. Kory
    D. Derrick
    E. Lily

Text #6

Before releasing a vehicle to customers
- All employees must wash their hands
- All employees must inspect the outside of the vehicle for scratches
- If the customer rejects a vehicle, report it to department O
- Ensure customer signs all paperwork

Upon return of the vehicle, employees must:

- Inspect all vehicles for cosmetic damage. If there is exterior damage, then report it to department Q
- Turn the vehicle on; if the engine does not start or there is a knocking sound, report it to department B
- If the vehicle is brought back with a flat tire, then tell depart S
- Ensure customer signs paperwork for the return of the vehicle.
- All employees must sign out at the end of the day

Managers

- Managers should be called any time there is a disgruntled customer.
- Managers should open and close the vault at the start and end of each shift.
- Crimes should be reported to the police.

21. Which statement is not true?
    A. Ensure the customer signs all paperwork
    B. Inspect the vehicle for cosmetic damage
    C. Check the tire pressure
    D. If the customer rejects a vehicle, notify department O
    E. Notify department B if the engine doesn't start

22. If the outside of a car door has a scratch, then what happens?
   A. Department Q is notified
   B. Nothing
   C. Department S is notified
   D. Department B is notified
   E. Department O is notified

23. When should the manager be called?
   A. For a lost vault combo
   B. Vehicle damage
   C. Engine trouble
   D. When Department Q is notified
   E. When a customer is angry

24. When is department B called?
   A. For a flat tire
   B. When a customer is upset
   C. When a customer rejects a vehicle
   D. When engine knocking is heard
   E. When the police are called

Text #7

Departments compensate employees according to the following incentive plan.

	First Customer Service Award	Second Customer Service Award	Performance Award	Employee of the Quarter
Sales	$100 1 day off	$250 3 days off	$500 1 week off	$1,000 2 weeks off
Human Resources	$100	$250 1 day off	$300 2 days off	$500 2 days off
Arts & Graphics	$150	$300 1 day off	$350 2 days off	$500 3 days off
IT	$100	$200 1 day off	$300 1 day off	$400 1 day off
Management	N/A	N/A	$2,000	N/A

25. Joe was designated as the employee of the quarter; however he did not receive any monetary benefits or time off. What department is Joe in?
   A. Sales
   B. Human Resources
   C. Arts & Graphics
   D. IT
   E. Management

26. Meghann received 2 days off and $300. What was she recognized for?
   A. First customer service award
   B. Second customer service award
   C. Performance
   D. Employee of the quarter
   E. Employee of the year

27. Which department has the largest monetary award for customer service?
   A. Sales
   B. Human Resources
   C. Arts & Graphics
   D. IT
   E. Management

28. Yogesh takes a 2-week trip with the time off he has been awarded. What has Yogesh most likely been recognized for?
   A. First customer service award
   B. Second customer service award
   C. Performance
   D. Employee of the quarter
   E. Employee of the year

Text #8

Tim, Abbey, and Kiley go to the grocery store. While at the store, they see Jill and Farid. Tim bought twice as many apples as Kiley. Abbey did not buy as many apples as Tim. Abbey bought more apples than Farid and the most apples among the girls. Of the five members in the group, two are girls, Abbey and Jill. One of the girls bought the least number of apples. Just considering apples purchased by the boys, Farid neither bought the most or least number of apples.

29. Who bought the least number of apples?
    A. Farid
    B. Jill
    C. Kiley
    D. Abbey
    E. Tim

30. Who bought the most amount of apples?
    A. Farid
    B. Jill
    C. Kiley
    D. Abbey
    E. Tim

31. Who bought the third greatest number of apples?
    A. Farid
    B. Jill
    C. Kiley
    D. Abbey
    E. Tim

32. Which boy bought the least number of apples?
    A. Farid
    B. Jill
    C. Kiley
    D. Abbey
    E. Tim

Text #9

The tallest buildings on each continent are arranged in the table below by continent, country, and city in no particular order.

Continent	Country	City
Asia	UAE	Dubai
Australia	Australia	Oceania
North America	United States	New York City
South America	Chile	Santiago
Europe	Russia	Saint Petersburg
Africa	South Africa	Johannesburg

The Carlton Center is located in Johannesburg. Q1 in Australia is taller than the building in Santiago but shorter than the tallest building in Asia, the Burj Khalifa. Lakhta in Russia is taller than the building in Oceania. One World Trade Center in the United States is taller than Q1. Africa has the shortest building. The Gran Torre is located in Chile. The building in Saint Petersburg is shorter than One World Trade Center.

33. What is the second tallest building?
    A. Burj Khalifa
    B. One World Trade Center
    C. Carlton Center
    D. Lakhta
    E. Q1

34. Which building is taller than Lakhta?
    A. The building in North America
    B. The building in Saint Petersburg
    C. Q1
    D. Gran Torre
    E. The building in Chile

35. Of the options below, which is located in South America?
    A. Johannesburg
    B. Oceania
    C. Carlton Center
    D. Gran Torre
    E. Q1

36. What building is shorter than the Gran Torre?
    A. Q1
    B. Lakhta
    C. Carlton Center
    D. The building in Oceania
    E. One World Trade center

Text #10

Dacks and Sam are brothers who like to play video games. They prefer to play Age of the Universe together. Stella plays CastleNight. Sam will play Eliquis while Dacks enjoys playing Tetrix with Jin when the brothers aren't playing together. Jin sometimes plays air hockey with Dustin. On the weekends, Dacks, Sam, and Dustin like to play football. Dustin will play Tetrix but prefers to play Aligarh with Jin. Jin also likes to play CastleNight but does not play with Stella.

37. Dacks and Jin are playing together. What game are they playing?
    A. Football
    B. Aligarh
    C. Age of the Universe
    D. Tetrix
    E. Eliquis

38. Dustin, Sam, and Dacks are playing together. What day of the week is it?
    A. Sunday
    B. Monday
    C. Tuesday
    D. Wednesday
    E. Thursday

39. Who is the only individual that does not play a game with at least one other person?
    A. Dacks
    B. Sam
    C. Stella
    D. Jin
    E. Dustin

40. When Dacks and Jin are playing together, what game is Sam most likely to play?
     A. CastleNight
     B. Aligarh
     C. Tetrix
     D. Air Hockey
     E. Eliquis

Numerical Reasoning – Part I

You are not allowed to use a calculator however, you will be able to use scratch paper to work out the problems.

41. Calculate $34.25 - 28.56$
     A. 3.21
     B. 4.59
     C. 5.69
     D. 6.18
     E. 7.48

42. Calculate $\frac{2}{3} \times \frac{4}{8}$
     A. $\frac{1}{4}$
     B. $\frac{1}{3}$
     C. $\frac{4}{6}$
     D. $\frac{16}{18}$
     E. $\frac{24}{28}$

43. Calculate $44712 \div 72$
     A. 289
     B. 318
     C. 451
     D. 575
     E. 621

44. $5x - 6 = 3x - 8$ What is the value of x?

A. -1
B. 1
C. 2.5
D. 3
E. 3.5

handwritten: $-3x$
handwritten: $2x - 6 = -8$
handwritten: $+6$
handwritten: $2x = -2$
handwritten: $x = -1$

45. Calculate $22.86 + 19.41$

A. 34.28
B. 36.79
C. 37.27
D. 42.27
E. 44.56

46. $9^x = 27^2$ What is the value of x?

A. 2
B. 3
C. 4
D. 5
E. 6

47. Calculate $18 + (36 \div 3^2)$

handwritten: multiply / divide before adding / subtracting.

A. 16
B. 18
C. 20
D. 22
E. 24

handwritten: $36 \div 9$
handwritten: $18 + 9 = 22$

48. Convert 0.56 to a fraction

A. $\dfrac{7}{9}$
B. $\dfrac{10}{18}$
C. $\dfrac{14}{25}$
D. $\dfrac{18}{38}$
E. $\dfrac{21}{31}$

49. Calculate 217×48

ends in 56 so answer in E.

    A. 689
    B. 714
    C. 821
    D. 973
    E. 10416

50. $2^{x+3} = 4^{x-2}$ What is the value of x?

- write equivalent expression.

    A. 3
    B. 4
    C. 5
    D. 6
    E. 7

51. Convert $\dfrac{3}{15}$ to a decimal

Long division

$$\frac{3}{15} \rightarrow 15\overline{)3.0} \rightarrow 0.2$$

    A. 0.2
    B. 0.25
    C. 0.3
    D. 0.35
    E. 0.4

52. Calculate $\dfrac{1}{4} + \dfrac{4}{5}$

    A. $\dfrac{3}{5}$
    B. $\dfrac{5}{9}$
    C. $\dfrac{7}{13}$
    D. $\dfrac{16}{19}$
    E. $\dfrac{21}{20}$

53. $\dfrac{5}{8} = \dfrac{x}{24}$ What is the value of x?

   A. 9
   B. 11
   C. 13
   D. 15
   E. 18

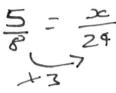

$\dfrac{5}{8} = \dfrac{x}{24}$

$\times 3$

So $x = 5 \times 3 = 15$

54. Calculate $\dfrac{1}{3} \div \dfrac{4}{3}$

   A. $\dfrac{1}{4}$
   B. $\dfrac{4}{9}$
   C. $\dfrac{5}{12}$
   D. $\dfrac{11}{9}$
   E. $\dfrac{15}{12}$

55. Calculate 1458×256

   A. 81637
   B. 89264
   C. 92567
   D. 156891
   E. 373248

56. Calculate $1895.478 - 65.29$

   A. 1632.459
   B. 1718.234
   C. 1830.188
   D. 1956.271
   E. 2016.58

57. $12 + 2x + 18 = 10$ What is the value of x?

   A. -10
   B. -5
   C. 1
   D. 5
   E. 10

58. Convert $\frac{5}{8}$ to a decimal

- eliminate
- guess

$\frac{5}{8}$ is one half
so likely D.

    A. 0.125
    B. 0.375
    C. 0.5
    D. 0.625 ⟵
    E. 0.875

59. Calculate 9.8×3.7

9.8×3.7

9.8
$\times 3.7$

    A. 34.51
    B. 36.26
    C. 38.59
    D. 40.74
    E. 42.18

60. Calculate $8 + (2 \times 5) \times 3^3 \div 9$

multiply / divide 1st
add - subtract 2nd

    A. 30
    B. 32
    C. 34
    D. 36
    E. 38

61. $\frac{6 - 3x}{4x} = \frac{-1}{2}$ What is the value of x?

    A. 4
    B. 6
    C. 8
    D. 10
    E. 12

62. Calculate $\frac{4}{8} + 4\frac{1}{2}$

$\frac{4}{8} = \frac{1}{2}$

    A. 5
    B. 5.5
    C. 6
    D. 6.5
    E. 7

A

Trick do 24 ÷ 24 so will be 3 and etc.

63. Convert $\frac{9}{24}$ to a decimal

A. 0.165
B. 0.375
C. 0.416
D. 0.583
E. 0.615

64. Calculate $\frac{1}{2} \div \frac{1}{6}$ $\rightarrow \frac{1}{2} \times \frac{6}{1}$

A. 3
B. 3.5
C. 4
D. 4.5
E. 5

65. Calculate 9.8×2.5

A. 18.75
B. 20
C. 22.25
D. 24.5
E. 26.75

Numerical Reasoning – Part II

You will be shown a graph or table and asked several questions relating to the information in the figure. Choose the best answer for each of the questions.

Chart #1

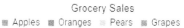

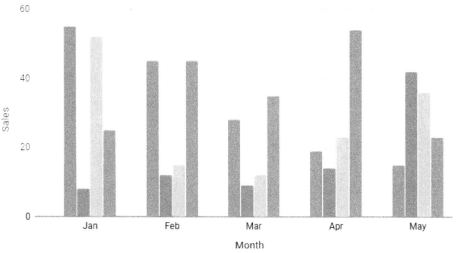

66. Which product is declining in sales?
    A. Apples
    B. Oranges
    C. Pears
    D. Grapes
    E. None of the Above

67. Which month had the largest increase in orange sales?
    A. Jan
    B. Feb
    C. Mar
    D. Apr
    E. May

68. In which month did Grape sales decrease by almost 50%
    A. Jan
    B. Feb
    C. Mar
    D. Apr
    E. May

69. In March, the company also sold lemons. The number of lemons sold
    was half the total number of Oranges sold between Jan-May. How
    many lemons were sold?
    A. 20
    B. 30
    C. 40
    D. 70
    E. 90

Chart #2

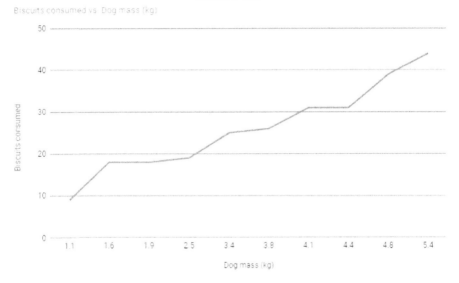

70. What is the difference in the dogs starting and ending weight?
    A. 3.2
    B. 4.3
    C. 12.6
    D. 36
    E. 48

71. How many biscuits were consumed when the dog's mass was 4.1kg?
    A. 12
    B. 18
    C. 25
    D. 31
    E. 38

72. What is the difference in the number of biscuits eaten between 4.1 and 2.5 kg?
    A. 4
    B. 8
    C. 12
    D. 25
    E. 50

73. What is the most likely number of biscuits consumed by a 5.8 kg dog?
    A. 20
    B. 30
    C. 35
    D. 40
    E. 50

Chart #3

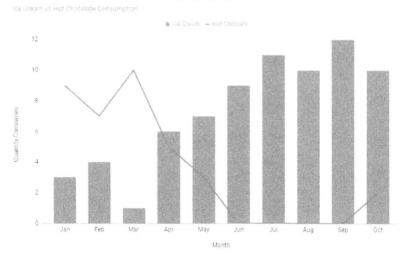

74. There is a correlation between the average monthly temperature and the quantity of ice cream consumed. The higher the monthly temperature, the more ice cream that is consumed. Based on the graph, which month was the hottest?
    A. Jan
    B. Mar
    C. Jul
    D. Sep
    E. Oct

75. How much hot chocolate was consumed in May?
    A. 0
    B. 2
    C. 3
    D. 5
    E. 7

76. During January, how much more hot chocolate was consumed than ice cream?
    A. 3
    B. 5
    C. 6
    D. 8
    E. 9

77. In which month was there twice as much ice cream consumed compared to the quantity of hot chocolate consumed in October?
    A. Feb
    B. Apr
    C. Jun
    D. Aug
    E. Sep

Chart #4

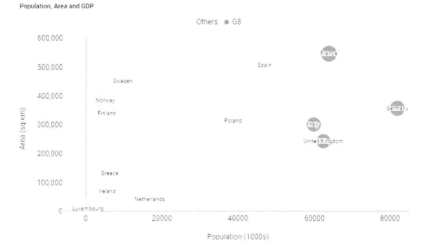

Population, Area and GDP

Others ● G8

78. Which G8 country is larger in area than Sweden?
    A. Spain
    B. Italy
    C. France
    D. United Kingdom
    E. Germany

79. Considering only the options below. Which of the below countries'
    populations differs the most compared to the others?
    A. Netherlands
    B. Ireland
    C. Greece
    D. Finland
    E. Norway

80. The size of the dots represents the relative magnitude of each
    country's Gross Domestic Product (GDP). Which country has the
    largest GDP?
    A. Germany
    B. France
    C. United Kingdom
    D. Sweden
    E. Luxembourg

81. Which country is half the total area of Spain?
    A. Poland
    B. United Kingdom
    C. Finland
    D. Greece
    E. Germany

Chart #5

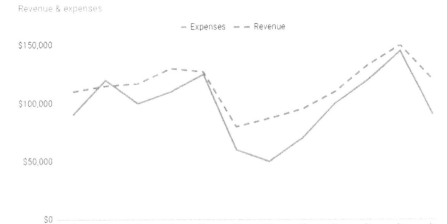

Revenue & expenses

— Expenses — — Revenue

$150,000

$100,000

$50,000

$0

January February March April May June July August September October November December

82. In which month did expenses elapse revenue?
    A. January
    B. February
    C. May
    D. July
    E. November

83. Approximate the difference between revenue and expenses during July?
    A. $20,000
    B. $40,000
    C. $80,000
    D. $120,000
    E. $140,000

84. Which month had the largest decline in revenue?
    A. March
    B. April
    C. May
    D. June
    E. July

85. In which month did revenue decrease while expenses increased when compared to the month prior?
   A. January
   B. April
   C. May
   D. August
   E. November

Chart #6

Train Number	Union Station	L'Enfant	Crystal City	Alexandria	Franconia / Springfield	Lorton	Woodbridge	Rippon	Quantico	Brooke L.
Amtrak* 67/65	7:20 a.m.			7:35 a.m.					8:04 a.m.	
301 S B	12:55 p.m.	1:03 p.m.	1:10 p.m.	1:18 p.m.	1:29 p.m.	1:36 p.m.	1:44 p.m.	1:50 p.m.	2:02 p.m.	2:21 p.m.
Amtrak* 95	2:30 p.m.			2:48 p.m.			3:05 p.m.		3:16 p.m.	
303	3:10 p.m.	3:18 p.m.	3:25 p.m.	3:33 p.m.	3:44 p.m.	3:51 p.m.	3:59 p.m.	4:05 p.m.	4:17 p.m.	4:36 p.m.
305 S	3:25 p.m.	3:33 p.m.	3:40 p.m.	3:48 p.m.	3:59 p.m.	4:06 p.m.	4:14 p.m.	4:20 p.m.	4:32 p.m.	4:51 p.m.
Amtrak* 125	3:55 p.m.	4:01 p.m.		4:14 p.m.			4:32 p.m.		4:45 p.m.	
307	4:10 p.m.	4:18 p.m.	4:25 p.m.	4:33 p.m.	4:44 p.m.	4:51 p.m.	4:59 p.m.	5:05 p.m.	5:17 p.m.	5:36 p.m.
309 S	4:40 p.m.	4:48 p.m.	4:55 p.m.	5:03 p.m.	5:14 p.m.	5:21 p.m.	5:29 p.m.	5:35 p.m.	5:47 p.m.	6:06 p.m.
311 B	5:15 p.m.	5:23 p.m.	5:30 p.m.	5:38 p.m.	5:49 p.m.	5:56 p.m.	6:04 p.m.	6:10 p.m.	6:22 p.m.	6:41 p.m.
Amtrak* 93	5:50 p.m.	5:55 p.m.		6:09 p.m.					6:37 p.m.	
313 S B	6:00 p.m.	6:08 p.m.	6:15 p.m.	6:23 p.m.	6:34 p.m.	6:41 p.m.	6:49 p.m.	6:55 p.m.	7:05 p.m.	7:19 p.m.
315 B	6:40 p.m.	6:48 p.m.	6:55 p.m.	7:03 p.m.	7:14 p.m.	7:21 p.m.	7:29 p.m.	7:35 p.m.	7:45 p.m.	7:59 p.m.
Amtrak* 85	7:05 p.m.			7:22 p.m.			7:40 p.m.		7:52 p.m.	

S	Special schedules for holidays and snow days.
B	Trains that allow full-size bicycles. Collapsible bicycles are permitted on all trains.
L	Trains may depart when station work is completed, regardless of scheduled time.

86. If you are traveling with a full-size bicycle, what is the latest you can leave Alexandria in order to arrive in Brooke before 7:25 p.m.?
   A. 5:38 p.m.
   B. 6:09 p.m.
   C. 6:23 p.m.
   D. 7:03 p.m.
   E. 7:22 p.m.

87. How many different trains could you take to get to Rippon?
   A. 7
   B. 8
   C. 9
   D. 10
   E. 11

88. If Dan leaves Lorton on the 303 train and Sarah leaves L'Enfant on the 307 train. How long will Dan wait at Brooke for Sarah to arrive?
    A. 60 min
    B. 68 min
    C. 71 min
    D. 75 min
    E. 78 min

89. Which train has the shortest transit time between Union Station and Woodbridge?
    A. Amtrak 67/65
    B. Amtrak 95
    C. 309
    D. 313
    E. Amtrak 85

Chart #7

Item	Current Inventory	Price for 1	Price when buying 3 or more
Apples	5	£ 1.25	£ 1.20
Oranges	4	£ 0.80	£ 0.75
Grapes	6	£ 5.50	£ 5.25
Lemons	12	£ 0.50	£ 0.40
Pears	8	£ 1.50	£ 1.25
Bananas	2	£ 0.25	£ 0.20

90. For which item is it not currently possible to receive a discounted price of three or more?
    A. Apples
    B. Oranges
    C. Grapes
    D. Pears
    E. Bananas

91. Rick buys 2x grapes, 3x pears, 1x apple, and 3x oranges. How much did he spend?
    A.   £ 16.00
    B.   £ 17.50
    C.   £ 18.25
    D.   £ 19.75
    E.   £ 20.00

92. Cedric has £26.00. He purchases 3x oranges, 1x banana, and 2x grapes. How much money does he have left?
    A.   £ 11.25
    B.   £ 12.50
    C.   £ 13.50
    D.   £ 14.75
    E.   £ 15.25

93. If the price for 1x orange is reduced by 25%. How much would 2x oranges now cost?
    A.   £ 0.20
    B.   £ 0.60
    C.   £ 0.80
    D.   £ 1.00
    E.   £ 1.20

94. What is the total quantity of products in inventory?
    A.   26
    B.   30
    C.   34
    D.   37
    E.   41

95. The store receives cherries. A bag of cherries costs half the price of 1x grape. The price for 3 or more cherries is the cost of a single bag of cherries minus the cost of 1x banana. What do 3 or more cherries cost?
    A.   £ 2.50
    B.   £ 2.75
    C.   £ 3.00
    D.   £ 3.25
    E.   £ 3.50

Work Rate

Each question shows a grid containing numbers, letters, and symbols. You will be given an original code made up of three letters or three numbers. Each letter or number is taken from a separate column in the grid.
In each question you will be given five alternative codes labelled (A –E . You have to decide which one of these alternative codes contains items taken from the same columns, and in the same order, as the original code.
Remember, during the actual test, you will have only 4 minutes to answer 20 questions.

96. Which could be an alternative code for KDB?

K	D	I	B
3	9	6	0
&	%	)	!

A. 3 % 0
B. 9) !
C. & % 6
D. 6 0 &
E. %) 0

97. Which could be an alternative code for TFU?

N	U	T	F
5	8	6	3
^	$	@	*

A. 8 @ *
B. 6 8 *
C. @ 3 8
D. 5 * $
E. ^ 8 3

98. Which could be an alternative code for 946?

6	9	2	4
F	Y	E	R
■	☐	🔓	◇

A. F ? R
B. Y E ?
C. ? E F
D. Y ? ?
E. E ? Y

99. Which could be an alternative code for 925?

5	2	9	7
A	Z	T	E
◖	⌘	◠	★

A. Z ⊙ ◖

B. ◠ ⌘ A

C. T ◖ ⊙

D. ⌘ A E

E. ZA ⊙

100. Which could be an alternative code for GQP?

G	C	Q	P
9	3	6	1
⩲	ⵣ	◆	✿

A. 3 ◆ 1
B. ⩲ 1 ✿

C. 9 ✦ ✿

D. 13 ✳

E. ✿ ✦ ✳

101. Which could be an alternative code for 102?

1	7	0	2
V	Z	L	K
⸬	⌣	✕	⟳

A. V ✕ K

B. Z ✕ V

C. ⸬ Z L

D. V ⟳ ✕

E. K ⌣ V

102. Which could be an alternative code for 067?

6	4	7	0
U	I	C	B
〒	﹨	+	⊥

A. B I +

B. ⊥ U C

C. I ﹨ U

D. 〒 B I

E. C I +

103. Which could be an alternative code for 132?

5	1	3	2
S	D	J	E
♠	♋	♡	✓

A. S J ✔

B. D ♡ ❧
C. J ♡ S
D. ☺ ✔ J
E. D ♡ E

104. Which could be an alternative code for ACX?

A	T	C	X
5	2	3	1
⊛	▲	♂	☽

A. 5 ▲ A
B. ⚘ ⚡ 1
C. ▲ 5 ☽
D. ⚡ 2 5
E. 1 3 ⚘

105. Which could be an alternative code for 521?

5	2	1	6
V	B	H	U
◖	❋	◇	=

A. ◖ B ◇
B. V H =
C. H V ❋
D. = ◖ B
E. ◇ B V

106. Which could be an alternative code for IZK?

K	I	Y	Z
9	3	6	1
▦	#	@	▶

A. 9 # 1

B. 3 @ 9

C. 1 ▦ 3

D. # ▶ 9

E. @ ▶ ▦

107. Which could be an alternative code for FVT?

F	T	Y	V
2	6	0	1
≫	♣	⊣	+

A. 2 ▯ +

B. ▯ 1 ▯

C. 0 + 2

D. 6 ⊣ +

E. ▯ 1 ▯

108. Which could be an alternative code for GER?

G	E	R	C
1	0	2	7
⬡	✿	◠	⊠

A. ◌0 2

B. 7 ▯ 1

C. ◠ ▯ 2

D. 1 7 ▯

E. 2 ⊠ 1

109. Which could be an alternative code for 678?

6	7	9	8
J	K	Z	Y
↺	⇧	✗	▶

A. K ↺ ➤
B. ↺ Z Y
C. J ⇧ ➤
D. Y ↺ ✗
E. ➤ Z K

110. Which could be an alternative code for MWR?

W	E	R	M
3	6	1	2
↳	◻	◢	☃

A. 3 ◢ ☃
B. ☃ 3 ◢
C. 6 ◢ ◻
D. 2 1 ◻
E. ◻ ◻ 2

111. Which could be an alternative code for IZV?

V	H	I	Z
3	0	4	5
@	!	%	&

A. 3 & 4
B. 5 4 !
C. @ % 0
D. ! 4 @
E. % 5 3

112. Which could be an alternative code for LCP?

P	L	Q	C
3	1	5	4
⊿	#	?	℧

A. 1 ? 4
B. 3 # ?
C. 1 5 ℧
D. # ℧ 3
E. 5 ⊿?

113. Which could be an alternative code for NTB?

B	N	T	U
1	8	9	2
⅄	θ	∧	|||

A. 8 ∧ ⅄
B. 9 |ı| 1
C. 1 θ 2
D. □ |ı| 8
E. ⅄ 9 8

114. Which could be an alternative code for 671?

1	7	4	6
N	U	J	K
⁎	⊙	~	∝

A. N J ∝
B. K ⊙ ⁎
C. J ≈ N

D. U ✳ J

E. ⊙ ∝U

115.　Which could be an alternative code for DFS?

G	S	D	F
2	8	7	4
⋈	∩	⊜	⋛

A. 7 8 ⋈
B. ∩ 4 2
C. ⊜ ⋛ 8
D. 2 4 ∩
E. ⋛ ⊜ 8

116.　Which could be an alternative code for 153?

1	2	5	3
B	U	E	W
⊘	⊯	{}	–○

A. U {} –○
B. E W ⊘
C. {} ⊯ B
D. ⊘ U W
E. B E –○

117.　Which could be an alternative code for ZEQ?

Q	Z	X	E
5	6	4	9
⊨	Δ	∞	Ā

A. Δ 9 5
B. ⊨ 4 Ā

C. 6 ∞ ⊨
D. 5 9 Δ
E. λ̄ ⊨ 4

118. Which could be an alternative code for 721?

7	3	1	2
P	T	C	M
Ψ	Θ	Σ	δ

A. T Σ δ
B. Ψ T N
C. P M Σ
D. Θ C P
E. Σ P C

119. Which could be an alternative code for 039?

9	0	5	3
B	C	J	L
◆	⊞	¥	☰

A. B ⊞ ☰
B. ⊞ ☰ B
C. C ¥ L
D. L ◆ ⊞
E. ☰ C ¥

120. Which could be an alternative code for YNE?

E	Y	C	N
5	7	1	2
£	€	$	¢

A. 5 € $

B. 2 1 £
C. 7 ¢ $
D. € ¢ 5
E. 1 2 5

121.　Which could be an alternative code for 419?

4	1	2	9
F	E	C	X
☀	¿	☺	☑

A. E ⊘ X
B. C ☑ ☀
C. X F ¿
D. ☀ C ☑
E. F ¿ X

122.　Which could be an alternative code for TAR?

A	R	T	C
9	8	3	2
┺	⊖	∂	★

A. A ∂ ★
B. ∂ 9 ⊖
C. ┺ 2 ⊖
D. 3 8 ┺
E. ⊖ ★ 9

123.　Which could be an alternative code for VKY?

Y	V	J	K
7	5	3	6
℘	∧	■	▽

A. ∧ ▽ 7

B. ∇ 3 ∞
C. 7 ■ 5
D. 6 ∇ ∞
E. ■ ∧ 6

124. Which could be an alternative code for DVS?

S	D	U	V
4	2	7	9
∄	≡	∓	⊛

A. 2 ∓ ⊛
B. 7 ∄ 2
C. ≡ ⊛ 4
D. ∄ ≡ 9
E. 2 ∓ 4

125. Which could be an alternative code for FYT?

Y	T	F	E
0	1	3	5
∴	±	÷	=

A. 0 ± =
B. ∴ ÷ 1
C. 3 5 ∴
D. 2 ± ÷
E. ÷ 0 ±

126. Which could be an alternative code for 971?

9	7	8	1
L	J	N	F
▲	◉	⊠	æ

A. L ☒ F

B. ▲ J æ

C. N L ⊙

D. ☒ F ▲

E. ⊙ N F

127. Which could be an alternative code for CHB?

B	C	A	H
8	2	4	1
웃	☀	✿	☠

A. 웃 4 ☠

B. ☀ 4 8

C. 1 ✿ 2

D. 2 ☠ 웃

E. 4 1 ☀

128. Which could be an alternative code for 035?

1	0	3	5
T	Y	H	V
☿	◆	☽	☯

A. T ◆ ☯

B. Y ☽ ☿

C. ☯ H Y

D. ☿ V ◆

E. ◆ H ☯

129. Which could be an alternative code for NXC?

B	N	C	X
8	4	2	6
⚝	↳	♡	♣

A. ↳ 8 6
B. 4 ☐ ♡
C. ⚝ 4 2
D. 6 ↳ 8
E. ♡ ☐ ⚝

130. Which could be an alternative code for 943?

4	7	3	9
K	L	H	T
♛	♪	►	★

A. ★ K ➤
B. L H ♛
C. ♪ T ➤
D. ♛ T L
E. L ★ K

131. Which could be an alternative code for XUQ?

Q	V	X	U
7	2	3	8
»	⚝	✿	♡

A. 7 ✿ ♡
B. 2 7 ✿
C. 3 ♡ 7
D. ⚝ ♡ »
E. 8 ⚝ 7

132. Which could be an alternative code for 895?

4	5	8	9
Y	T	O	P
↺	↴	✍	➤·

A. T ➤➤ ↺
B. O ↴ P
C. ✍ ↺ T
D. T Y P
E. O P ↴

133. Which could be an alternative code for MBN?

M	O	N	B
4	1	6	2
∞	☎	∀	◆

A. ∞ 2 6
B. 2 ∀ ◆
C. ☎ 4 2
D. 6 1 ∞
E. ∀ 6 4

134. Which could be an alternative code for 738?

8	1	7	3
R	M	B	T
≠	▲	☣	⠿

A. M ≠ ☣
B. T ▲ R
C. B M ⠿
D. ☣ T ≠

E. ⠒ ▲ R

135. Which could be an alternative code for 794?

4	7	1	9
G	R	W	H
⏀	∇	⊓	Σ

A. R W Σ
B. ∇ ⊓ H
C. R H ⏀
D. ∇ G W
E. ⏀ ⊓ R

Spatial Reasoning – Part I

In each question you will be shown three to four shapes that will have at least one side labeled x, y, or z. Place the sides with the same labels next to each other to form a new shape. Your task is to determine what the new joined together shape would look like.

136.

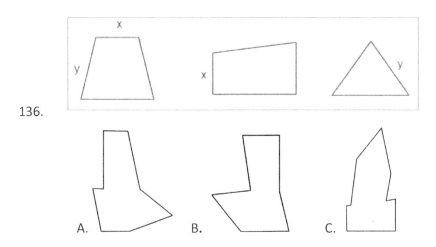

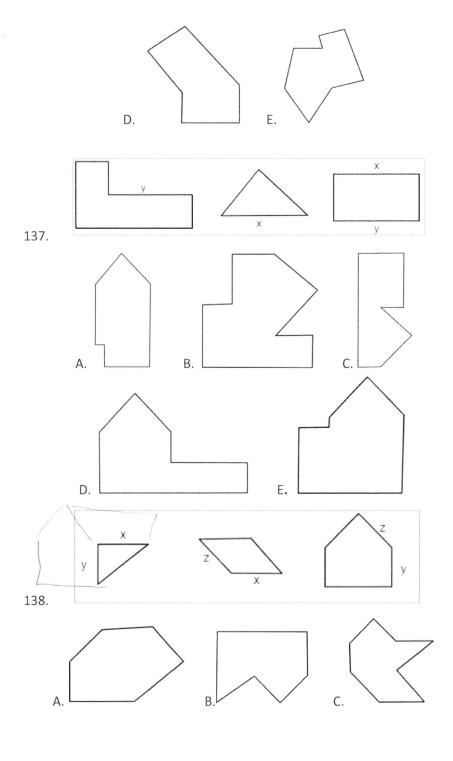

D.

E.

137.

A.

B.

C.

D.

E.

138.

A.

B.

C.

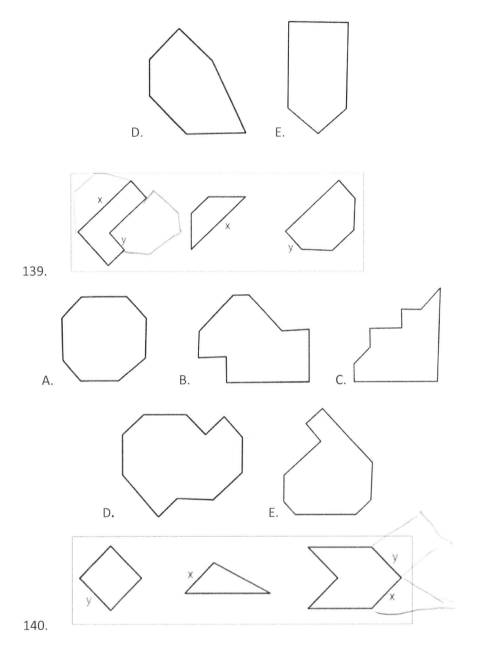

D.

E.

139.

A.

B.

C.

D.

E.

140.

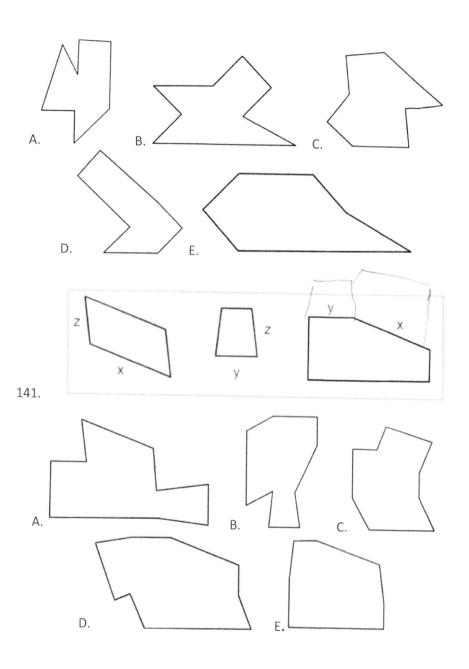

A.

B.

C.

D.

E.

z

x

z

y

y

x

141.

A.

B.

C.

D.

E.

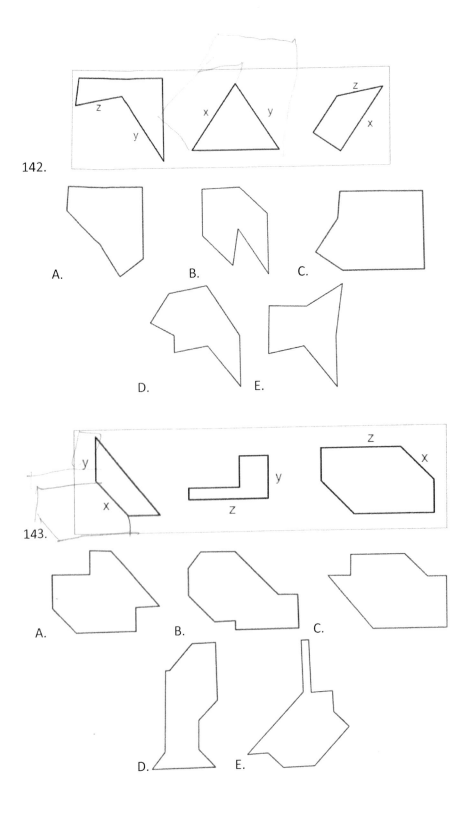

142.

A.

B.

C.

D.

E.

143.

A.

B.

C.

D.

E.

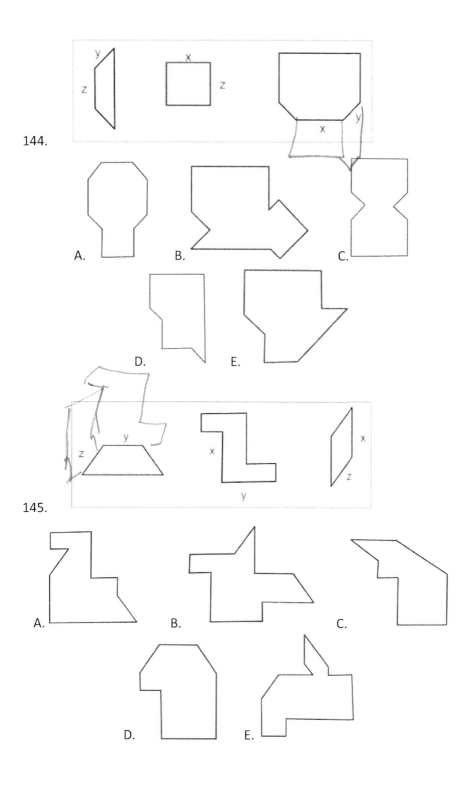

144.

y
z
x
z
x
y

A.
B.
C.
D.
E.

145.

y
z
x
x
z
y

A.
B.
C.
D.
E.

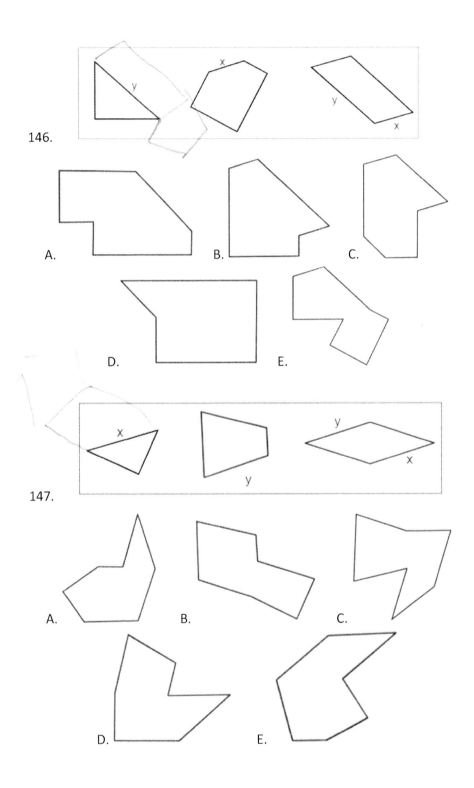

146.

A.

B.

C.

D.

E.

147.

A.

B.

C.

D.

E.

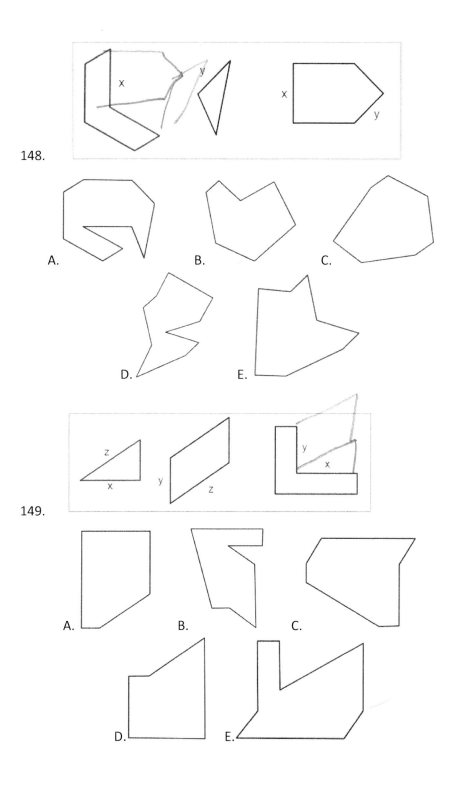

148.

A.

B.

C.

D.

E.

149.

A.

B.

C.

D.

E.

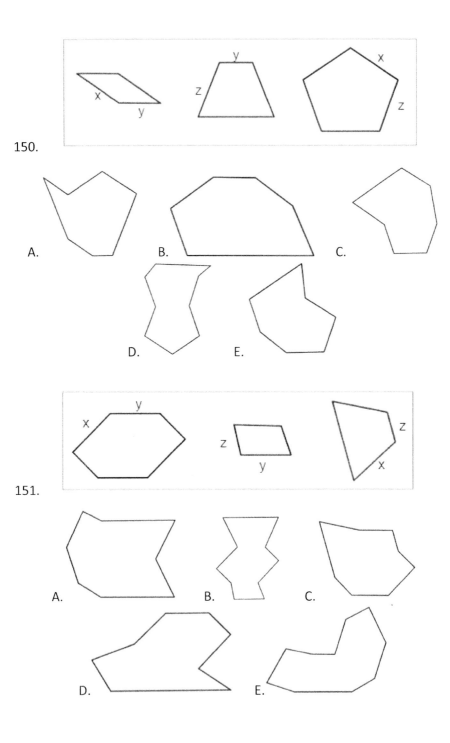

150.

A.

B.

C.

D.

E.

151.

A.

B.

C.

D.

E.

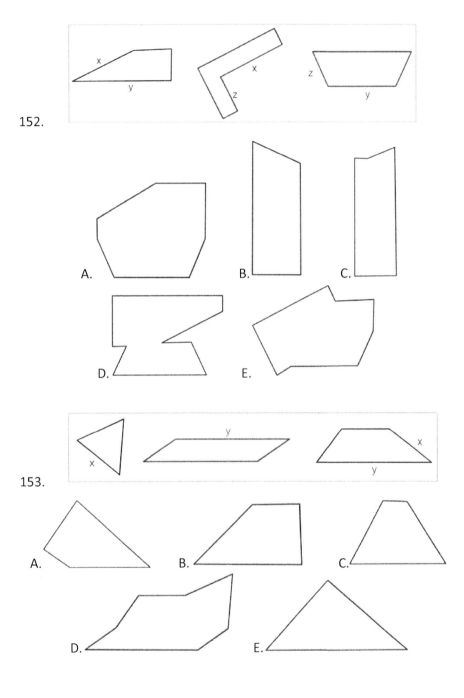

152.

A.   B.   C.

D.   E.

153.

A.   B.   C.

D.   E.

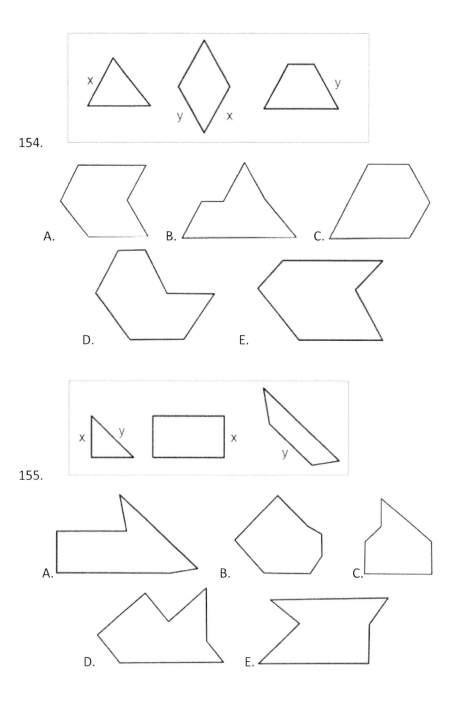

154.

A.

B.

C.

D.

E.

155.

A.

B.

C.

D.

E.

156.

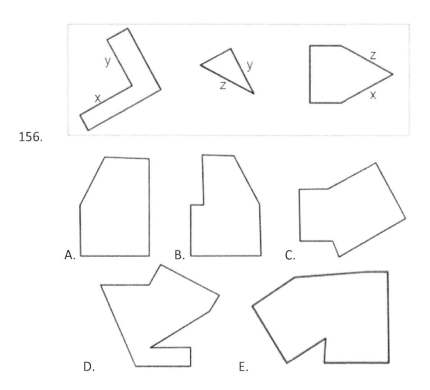

A.   B.   C.

D.   E.

Spatial Reasoning – Part II

In each question you will be shown two separate objects, each with a dot placed in one corner.

You will be shown the same two objects after each has been rotated in some way. You have to decide which option shows both rotated objects with the dot placed in the correct corner.

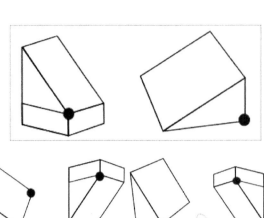

157.

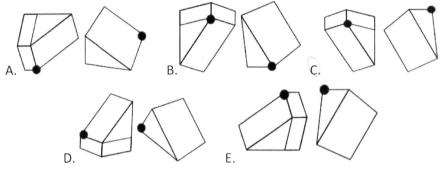

A. B. C.

D. E.

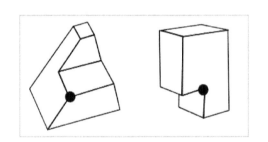

158.

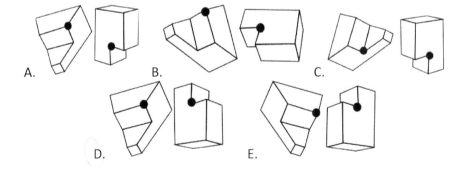

A. B. C.

D. E.

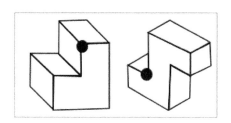

159.

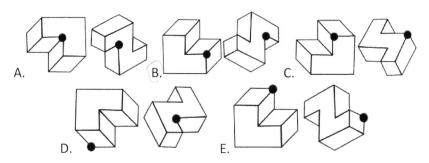

A. B. C.

D. E.

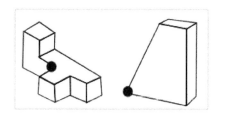

160.

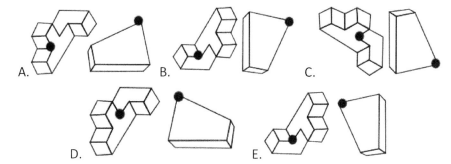

A. B. C.

D. E.

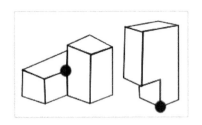

161.

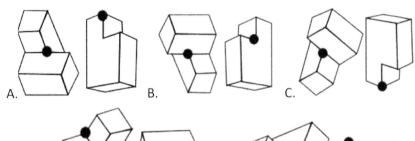

A.   B.   C.   D.

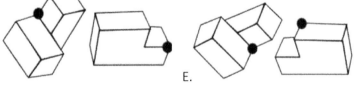

E.

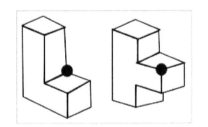

162.

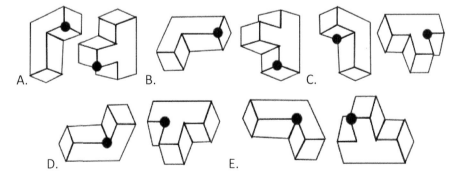

A.   B.   C.

D.   E.

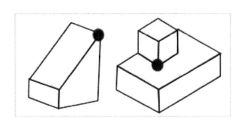

163.

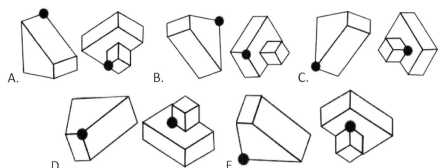

A. B. C.

D. E.

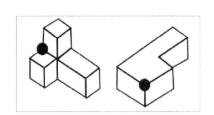

164.

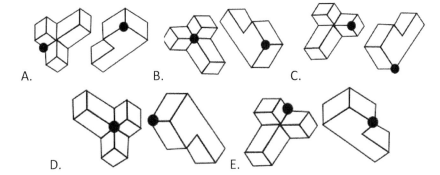

A. B. C.

D. E.

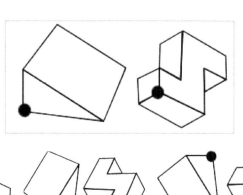

165.

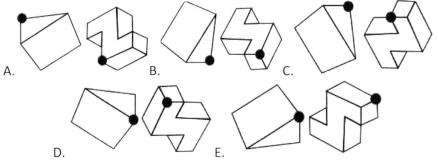

A.   B.   C.

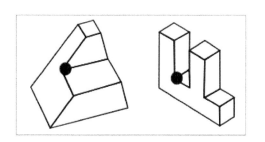

D.   E.

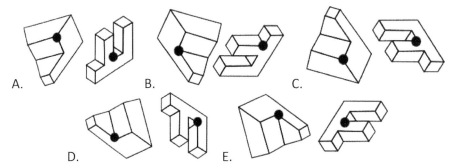

166.

A.   B.   C.

D.   E.

167.

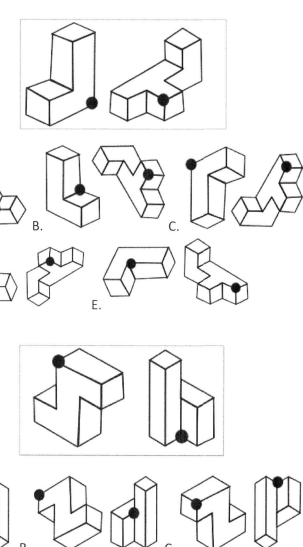

A.

B.

C.

D.

E.

168.

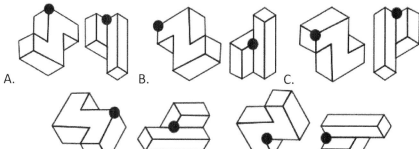

A.

B.

C.

D.

E.

169.

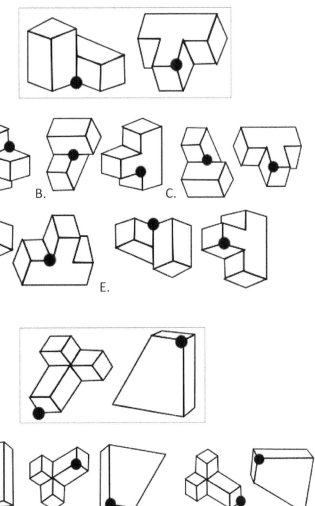

A.

B.

C.

D.

E.

170.

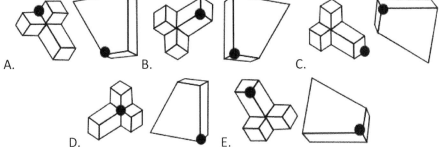

A.

B.

C.

D.

E.

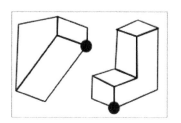

171.

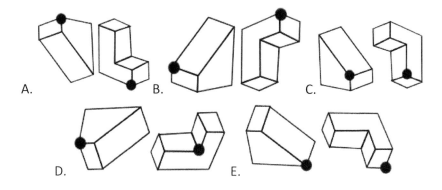

A. B. C.

D. E.

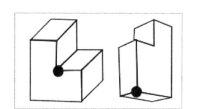

172.

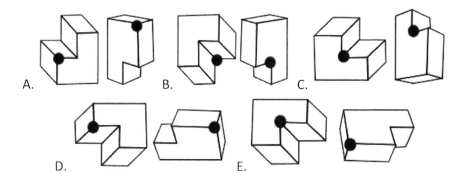

A. B. C.

D. E.

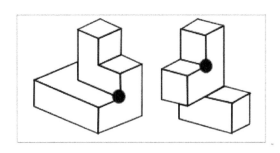

173.

174.

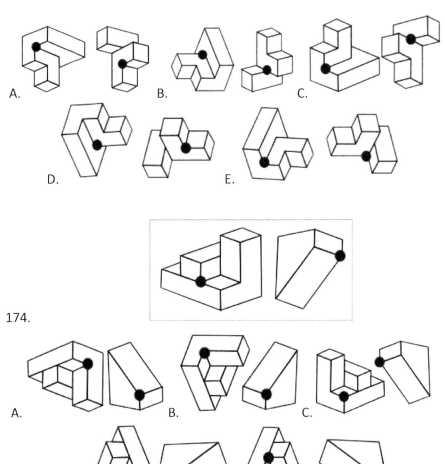

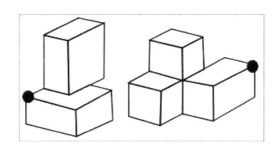

175.

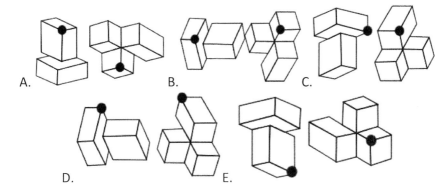

A. B. C.

D. E.

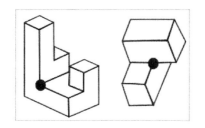

176.

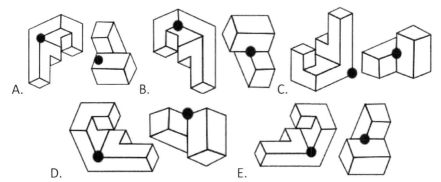

A. B. C.

D. E.

177.

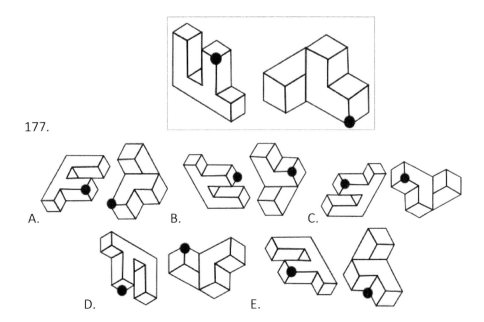

A. B. C.

D. E.

Electrical Comprehension

This section tests your ability to work with electrical concepts. Choose the best answer for each question.

178.   Which switch/switches must be closed in order to turn the light bulb on?

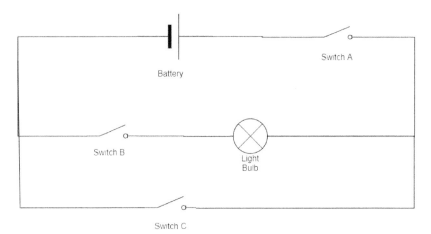

A. Switch A
B. Switch B and C
C. Switch A and C
D. Switch A and B
E. Switch B

179. Two 3V batteries are wired together as shown. What is the output voltage?

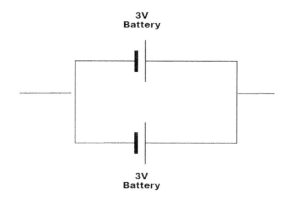

3V
Battery

3V
Battery

A. 1.5V
B. 3V
C. 6V
D. 9V
E. 12V

180. Which quantity has units of KWh?
A. Energy
B. Power
C. Charge
D. Current
E. Resistance

181. Ratings on fuses are expressed in which unit?
A. Ampere- hours
B. Volts
C. Volt-Ampere
D. KWh
E. Amperes

182.   A light is connected to a 12V source with a 4A current. Assuming
the wires produce no resistance, what is the resistance of the light?
A. 2 Ω
B. 3 Ω
C. 4 Ω
D. 6 Ω
E. 8 Ω

183.   What is the equivalent resistance of the following circuit?

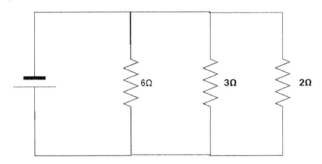

A. 1 Ω
B. 5 Ω
C. 9 Ω
D. 12 Ω
E. 24 Ω

184.   Four resistors are connected in series; each resistor has a value of
320 Ω. What is the total resistance?
A. 80 Ω
B. 320 Ω
C. 1280 Ω
D. 2560 Ω
E. 3200 Ω

185.   Suppose that the voltage in a circuit is doubled and the resistance
is reduced by half. What will happen to the current?
A. Current is quartered
B. Current is halved
C. Current is doubled
D. Current is quadrupled
E. Current remains the same

186.   What is the value of IR in the diagram?

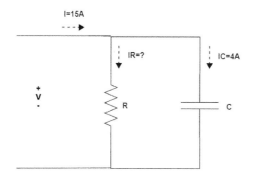

A. 4 A
B. 6 A
C. 11 A
D. 15 A
E. 19 A

187.   Farad is the SI unit of?
A. Impedance
B. Capacitance
C. Resistance
D. Inductance
E. Energy

188.   The characteristic of an electrical circuit to oppose any change in
current is known as?
A. Impedance
B. Capacitance
C. Resistance
D. Inductance
E. Energy

189.   What is the equivalent resistance of the circuit shown?

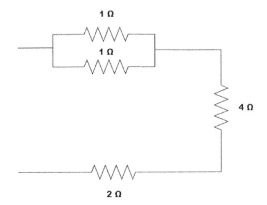

A.   1 Ω
B.   2 Ω
C.   4 Ω
D.   6 Ω
E.   8 Ω

190.   An ammeter is used to measure?
A.   Current
B.   Voltage
C.   Resistance
D.   Power
E.   Capacitance

191.   Batteries are connected in parallel in order to increase?
A.   Voltage
B.   Efficiency
C.   Battery life
D.   Inductance
E.   Amp-hour capacity

192.   If a short circuit occurred, then?
A.   A small amount of current flows
B.   A large amount of current flows
C.   No current flows
D.   Max power occurs
E.   Max charge occurs

193. Which resistor will have the largest drop in voltage?

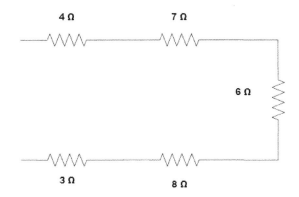

A. 3 Ω
B. 4 Ω
C. 6 Ω
D. 7 Ω
E. 8 Ω

194. Batteries are connected in series in order to increase?
A. Life of the battery
B. Efficiency
C. Voltage
D. Current
E. Capacitance

195. A resistor reduces?
A. Resistance
B. Current
C. Heat
D. Frequency
E. Cycle

196. What is the current if a charge of 10 Coulombs passes in 2 seconds?
A. 2 A
B. 4 A
C. 5 A
D. 8 A
E. 10 A

197.   In a battery, current flows in what direction?
   A. Positive to negative
   B. Negative to positive
   C. Cathode to anode
   D. Anode to negative
   E. Cathode to negative

198.   What is the supply voltage in the following diagram?

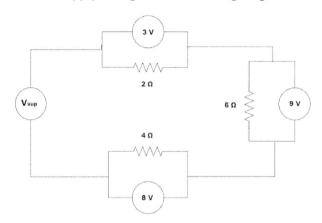

   A. 3 V
   B. 9 V
   C. 18 V
   D. 20 V
   E. 27 V

199.   In direct current
   A. Magnitude and direction remain constant
   B. Magnitude and direction change
   C. Only magnitude changes
   D. Only direction changes
   E. Magnitude and direction flip

200.   A 3 Ω resistor having a 2 A current will dissipate the power of?
   A. 1.5 W
   B. 3 W
   C. 6 W
   D. 9 W
   E. 12 W

201.   The purpose of an insulator is to?
        A.   Increase efficiency
        B.   Store current
        C.   Resist the flow of current
        D.   Conduct current
        E.   Increase capacitance

202.   If bulb number 1 goes out, how many bulbs will remain lit?

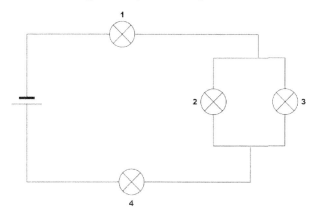

        A.   0
        B.   1
        C.   2
        D.   3
        E.   4

203.   The resistance of a wire varies inversely with?
        A.   Length
        B.   Power
        C.   Temperature
        D.   Cross section area
        E.   Resistivity

204.   A plastic rod when rubbed with a cloth becomes charged because?
        A.   The rod gives up protons
        B.   The rod gives up electrons
        C.   The rod takes protons
        D.   The rod gives up atoms
        E.   The rod takes atoms

205.   Electrical charged can be stored in?
        A. Inductor
        B. Diode
        C. Transistor
        D. Semiconductor
        E. Capacitor

206.   What device would you use to measure electrical resistance?
        A. Ohmmeter
        B. Ammeter
        C. Voltmeter
        D. Electrical meter
        E. Current meter

207.   What is the current in the ammeter?

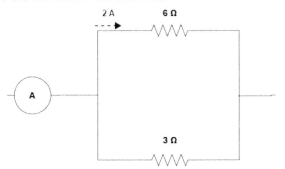

        A. 2 A
        B. 3 A
        C. 4 A
        D. 6 A
        E. 12 A

208.   If a single light bulb is removed from a circuit with three light bulbs
        in total, and the other two bulbs also go out, the lights must have been
        connected in _____ ?
        A. Parallel
        B. Open
        C. Series
        D. Closed
        E. Complex

209.   What device allows electricity to flow in one direction, but not the opposite direction?
   A. Inductor
   B. Diode
   C. Amplifier
   D. Transformer
   E. Switch

210.   If the voltage across a load is doubled and the resistance is reduced by half, what is the effect on the current, I?
   A. 0.5 I
   B. I
   C. 2 I
   D. 4 I
   E. 8 I

211.   What is the current in the circuit below?

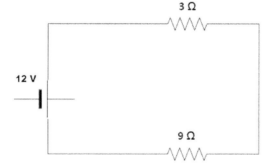

   A. 1 A
   B. 3 A
   C. 4 A
   D. 6 A
   E. 12 A

212.   If resistance increases 4 times and the current doubles, what happens to the voltage?
   A. 0.5 V
   B. 1 V
   C. 2 V
   D. 4 V
   E. 8 V

213.   A transformer?
       A.   Changes DC to AC
       B.   Changes AC to DC
       C.   Steps AC voltage up or down
       D.   Steps Ac and DC voltage up or down
       E.   Steps DC voltage up or down

214.   The SI unit for cycles per a second is?
       A.   Frequency
       B.   Hertz
       C.   Ampere
       D.   Coulomb
       E.   Farad

215.   What does the voltmeter read?

       A.   2 V
       B.   4 V
       C.   6 V
       D.   8 V
       E.   10 V

216.   Electrical power is measured in?
       A.   Watts
       B.   Volts
       C.   Amperes
       D.   Frequency
       E.   Coulomb

217.   Solid state devices are made from?
       A.   Conductive material
       B.   Insulating material
       C.   Conductive and insulating material
       D.   Entirely of semiconductor material
       E.   No semiconductor material

218.   3 amps is equivalent to how many milliamps?
    A. 0.003 mA
    B. 0.03 mA
    C. 30 mA
    D. 300 mA
    E. 3000 mA

219.   If one of the fuses blows, and none of the lamps light up, which fuse is blown?

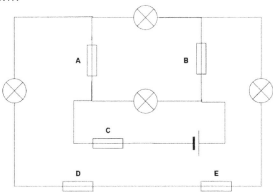

    A. A
    B. B
    C. C
    D. D
    E. E

220.   Inductors in series behave the same as?
    A. Resistors in parallel
    B. Resistors in series
    C. Capacitors in series
    D. Capacitors in parallel
    E. Inductors in parallel

221.   The property of a circuit to oppose any change in current is known as?
    A. Inductance
    B. Capacitance
    C. Resistance
    D. Impedance
    E. Power

222. Henry is the SI unit of?
    A. Inductance
    B. Capacitance
    C. Resistance
    D. Impedance
    E. Power

Mechanical Comprehension

This section tests your ability to work with mechanical concepts. Choose the best answer for each question.

223. Work happens when?
    A. Force cannot overcome resistance
    B. Force is applied
    C. Force is applied in a direction
    D. Force moves an object over a distance
    E. Force is removed

224. Weight is?
    A. Density of an object
    B. Forced exerted on an object due to gravity
    C. Mass of an object
    D. Gravity generated by an object
    E. Amount of matter in the object

225. A larger gear is turning a smaller gear. Which of the following does not occur with the smaller gear?
    A. Torque decreases
    B. Increase in rotational speed
    C. Change in gear ratio
    D. Change in rotational direction
    E. Change in speed

226.   What is the minimum amount of force required to lift the weight?

A.   100 N
B.   250 N
C.   500 N
D.   750 N
E.   1000 N

227.   A 8cm diameter axle turns a 64cm diameter wheel. What is the
mechanical advantage of the system?
A.   1:1
B.   2:1
C.   4:1
D.   6:1
E.   8:1

228.   9N of force is applied using a wrench that has a length of 0.5
meters. How much torque is generated?
A.   4.5 N·m
B.   9 N·m
C.   12.5 N·m
D.   18 N·m
E.   81 N·m

229.   A large gear has 24 teeth and is connected to a smaller gear with 8
teeth. If the larger wheel makes 12 revolutions, how many revolutions
will the smaller gear make?
A.   12
B.   18
C.   24
D.   36
E.   48

230. If gear 1 turns clockwise, what directions do bars X and Y move?

   A. Bar X moves right and bar Y moves left
   B. Bar X and Y both move right
   C. Bar X moves left and bar Y moves right
   D. Bar X and Y both move left
   E. Neither bar X or Y moves

231. A 10 kg object impacts a wall releasing 125 J of energy. What was the speed of the object before it impacted the wall?
   A. 3 m/s
   B. 5 m/s
   C. 10 m/s
   D. 15 m/s
   E. 20 m/s

232. An object is dropped from a height of 5 meters. When the ball hits the ground what is its approximate velocity?
   A. 5 m/s
   B. 9 m/s
   C. 10 m/s
   D. 20 m/s
   E. 32 m/s

233. When torque increases, speed?
   A. Decreases
   B. Remains the same
   C. Increases
   D. Increases, then decreases
   E. Decreases, then increases

234. A tank contains several cubic meters of water. (1 cubic meter of water = 1000kg). The tank is 50 meters deep, 10 meters wide, and 200 meters long. What is the approximate pressure the tank of water exerts on the ground?
   A. 20,000 N/m²
   B. 50,000 N/m²
   C. 100,000 N/m²
   D. 250,000 N/m²
   E. 500,000 N/m²

235. How much weight is required to balance the beam?

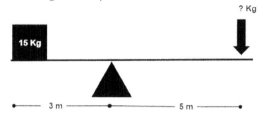

   A. 3 Kg
   B. 5 Kg
   C. 6 Kg
   D. 9 Kg
   E. 18 Kg

236. Water flows into a container at 120 liters per a minute. The bottom of the container has a hole which causes water to leak out at a rate of 1 liter per a second. How long will it take to fill the container with 210 liters of water?
   A. 3 minutes
   B. 3.5 minutes
   C. 4 minutes
   D. 4.5 minutes
   E. 5 minutes

237. The sideways force felt turning a sharp turn is called?
   A. Centrifugal force
   B. Thrust
   C. Angular force
   D. Gravity
   E. Positive force

238. What is power?
    A. Difference in resistance
    B. Energy of an object
    C. Rate of work
    D. Application of force
    E. Capacity to do work

239. What is energy?
    A. Rate of work
    B. Capacity to do work
    C. Opposition of weight
    D. Application of force
    E. Motion

240. A 10 N force compresses two identical springs arranged in series by 8 cm. If the same two springs are arranged in parallel instead of series what distance will the springs now be compressed?
    A. 2 cm
    B. 4 cm
    C. 6 cm
    D. 8 cm
    E. 10 cm

241. Wheels M and N have a diameter of 6 cm and wheels Y and Z have diameters of 3 cm. Wheels N and Y are attached to one another and rotate at the same rate. If wheel M makes one complete revolution how many revolutions does wheel Z make?

    A. One complete revolution
    B. Two complete revolutions
    C. Three complete revolutions
    D. Four complete revolutions
    E. Six complete revolutions

242.   An object falls to the ground from a height of 20 meters. What is the objects approximate velocity when it hits the ground?

    A. 5 m/s
    B. 10 m/s
    C. 20 m/s
    D. 25 m/s
    E. 30 m/s

243.   A 10 kg object stretches a spring vertically by 6 cm. If an additional 5 kg are added so the total is now 15 kg. How much will the spring stretch?

    A. 6 cm
    B. 7 cm
    C. 8 cm
    D. 9 cm
    E. 10 cm

244.   An engine produces 140 hp and is 85% efficient. How much horsepower is lost due to inefficiency?

    A. 6 hp
    B. 11 hp
    C. 15 hp
    D. 19 hp
    E. 21 hp

245.   A car accelerates from 15 m/s to 45 m/s in 2 seconds. What is the acceleration?

    A. 2 m/s^2
    B. 8 m/s^2
    C. 15 m/s^2
    D. 20 m/s^2
    E. 25 m/s^2

246.   Which of the following is a vector quantity?

    A. Velocity
    B. Speed
    C. Temperature
    D. Mass
    E. Energy

247. Bar F is fixed and the remaining bars are free to pivot at the joints. A force is applied in the upward direction at Z. What direction will points X and Y move?

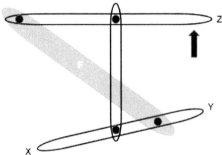

A. X and Y both move up
B. X moves up and Y moves down
C. X and Y both move down
D. X moves down and Y moves up
E. X and Y do not move

248. Hydraulic jacks exert force on an object using?
A. Compressed air
B. Compressed liquid
C. Incompressible liquid
D. Incompressible air
E. Compressed air and liquids

249. What is the name of the force that causes circular motion and in which direction does it act?
A. Centripetal force, acting in the direction of motion
B. Centrifugal force, acting towards the center
C. Centripetal force, acting away from the center
D. Centrifugal force, acting away from the center
E. Centripetal force, acting towards the center

250.   A small ball moving with a velocity of 2 m/s to the right collides elastically with a stationary bowling ball. After the collision, the bowling ball does not move. What is the velocity and direction of the small ball after the collision?

A.   0 m/s
B.   1 m/s to the left
C.   2 m/s to the right
D.   2 m/s to the left
E.   4 m/s to the left

251.   Two objects inelastically collide. Which of the following statements are true?

A.   Kinetic energy is conserved
B.   Kinetic energy is not conserved
C.   Kinetic energy is gained
D.   All kinetic energy transforms to thermal energy
E.   All kinetic energy transforms to potential energy

252.   A freight car has a mass of 24,000 kg and moves with a constant velocity of 8 m/s. The freight car collides with a stationary car carrier that has a mass of 8,000 kg. After the collision, the freight cars sticks together to the car carrier. What is the velocity of the two cars after the collision?

A.   2 m/s
B.   4 m/s
C.   6 m/s
D.   8 m/s
E.   12 m/s

253. If gear X turns clockwise with a constant speed of 12 rpm. How does gear Y turn if all gears are identical?

A. Counterclockwise and faster
B. Clockwise and slower
C. Clockwise and faster
D. Counterclockwise slower
E. Counterclockwise at 12 rpm

254. Shock absorbers on a car act like a spring. If a car hits a pothole with 600N of force and the shock absorber compresses 10cm. What is the spring constant?
A. 60 N/m
B. 200 N/m
C. 600 N/m
D. 6000 N/m
E. 8000 N/m

255. A force of 1500 N is applied to the base of a square pedestal that is 3 meters wide and 5 meters long. What is the pressure on the pedestal?
A. 100 Pa
B. 150 Pa
C. 1000 Pa
D. 1500 Pa
E. 10000 Pa

256.   Assume the vessel and pipes are entirely filled with water. How
will pressure Gage A compare to pressure Gage B?

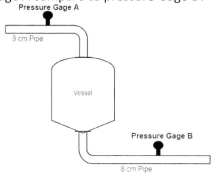

A.   A and B will be the same
B.   A will be higher than B
C.   B will be higher than A
D.   B will be less than A
E.   A and B will constantly fluctuate

257.   A ball is thrown into the air with 9 N of force. The ball travels 18
meters. How much work was done?
    A.   74 J
    B.   162 J
    C.   186 J
    D.   208 J
    E.   216 J

258.   Which of the following pairs are both vectors?
    A.   Area and time
    B.   Pressure and momentum
    C.   Acceleration and temperature
    D.   Energy and mass
    E.   Weight and force

259.   A force acts on an area to produce a pressure. Which change
produce the same original pressure?
    A.   Halve the area and double the force
    B.   Double the area and quadruple the force
    C.   Double the area and halve the force
    D.   Double the area and double the force
    E.   Halve the area and quadruple the force

260. If the atmospheric pressure increases. What distance also increases

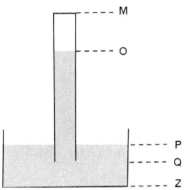

A. OZ
B. PQ
C. PZ
D. MO
E. QZ

261. Consider a gear train with 2 gears. Gear 1 has 20 teeth and Gear 2 has 80 teeth. If Gear 1 is turning clockwise at 40 RPM, what direction and speed does Gear 2 turn?
   A. 10 rpm, counter clockwise
   B. 10 rpm, clockwise
   C. 80 rpm, counter clockwise
   D. 80 rpm, clockwise
   E. 40 rpm, counter clockwise

Memory – Part I

During the test you will be shown a sequence of six to eight letters. The letters will be shown one at a time. You will have to remember the order in which they appear. You will then be shown two letters from the sequence.

Your task is to decide how many letters were shown between the two letters in the original sequence. In this section you will be given four options (A–D).

For practice, I recommend you memorize the letters and then cover them so you do not refer back to them while reading the question.

262.

E V R O P C

How many letters were shown between V and P?
A. 1
B. 2
C. 3
D. 4

263.

V C B N W K

How many letters were shown between V and B?
A. 1
B. 2
C. 3
D. 4

264.

D J Z Q H F

How many letters were shown between H and D?
A. 1
B. 2
C. 3
D. 4

265.

Y B V T N K U

How many letters were shown between U and B?
A. 2
B. 3
C. 4
D. 5

266.

C B X A Q R M

How many letters were shown between C and M?
A. 2
B. 3
C. 4
D. 5

267.

| A | S | D | E | Y | P | Z |

How many letters were shown between A and Z?
A. 4
B. 5
C. 6
D. 7

268.

| D | W | N | B | V | Y | U |

How many letters were shown between N and D?
A. 1
B. 2
C. 3
D. 4

269.

| G | J | S | U | W | Q |

How many letters were shown between J and W?
A. 2
B. 3
C. 4
D. 5

270.

| M | B | H | C | G | A |

How many letters were shown between A and B?
A. 1
B. 2
C. 3
D. 4

271.

| C | T | V | J | K | S | D | E |

How many letters were shown between T and S?
A. 2
B. 3
C. 4
D. 5

272.

K S E R W B C P

How many letters were shown between S and P?

A. 2
B. 3
C. 4
D. 5

273.

F V D U P Q

How many letters were shown between U and V?

A. 1
B. 2
C. 3
D. 4

274.

F L W E T P O

How many letters were shown between O and E?

A. 1
B. 2
C. 3
D. 4

275.

H D R Z B U C P

How many letters were shown between B and H?

A. 1
B. 2
C. 3
D. 4

276.

T X S F L K P E

How many letters were shown between T and E?

A. 3
B. 4
C. 5
D. 6

277. G H J E R U P

How many letters were shown between R and G?
A. 3
B. 4
C. 5
D. 6

278. E U V C A W

How many letters were shown between E and A?
A. 3
B. 4
C. 5
D. 6

279. L K T Z Q A O B

How many letters were shown between B and T?
A. 2
B. 3
C. 4
D. 5

280. P M O E R T S D

How many letters were shown between R and P?
A. 1
B. 2
C. 3
D. 4

281. U W V X C Z B A

How many letters were shown between U and X?
A. 1
B. 2
C. 3
D. 4

282.
| Y | Q | I | P | T | W | H | G |

How many letters were shown between H and Q?

A. 1
B. 2
C. 3
D. 4

Memory – Part II

This section tests your ability to recognize patterns. During the actual test you will be shown a sequence of two or three grids one at a time.

Squares in the grid will be filled in. You will then be asked to determine what a new grid would like if all the grids shown were added together. In this section you will be given four options (A–D).

For practice, I recommend you memorize the grids one at a time and then cover them so you do not subconsciously refer back to the original grids while reading the question.

283.

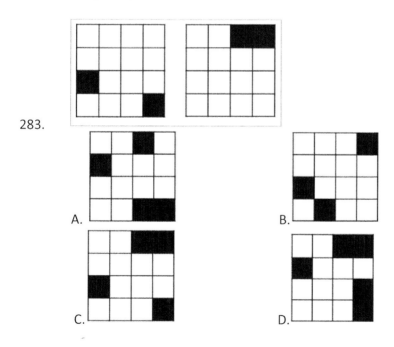

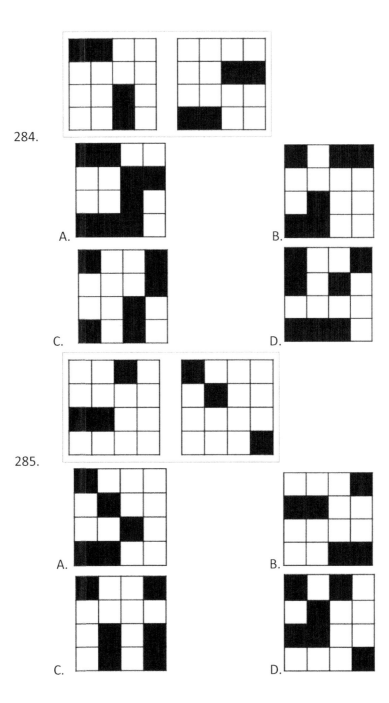

284.

A.　　　B.

C.　　　D.

285.

A.　　　B.

C.　　　D.

286.

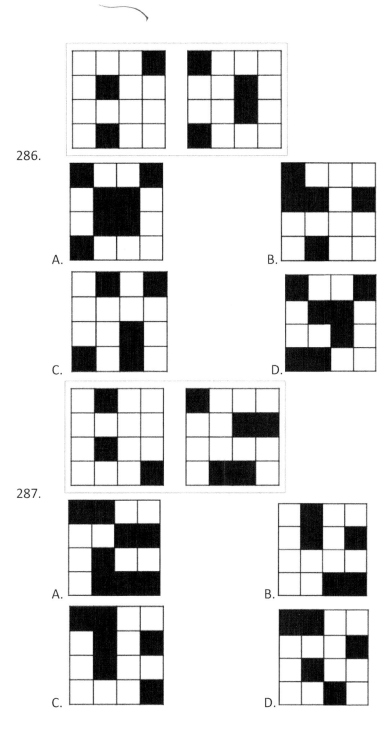

287.

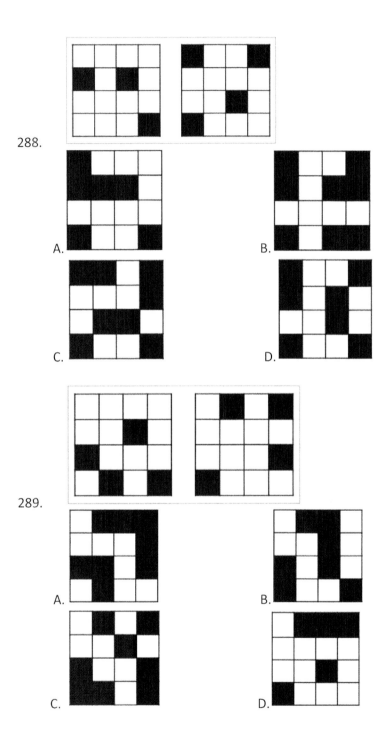

288.

289.

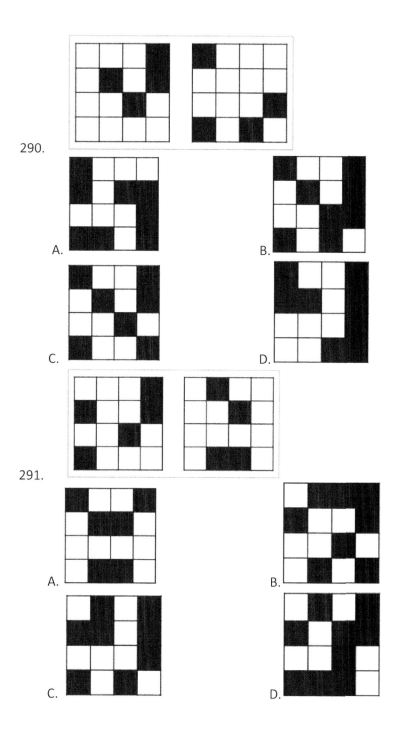

290.

A.

B.

C.

D.

291.

A.

B.

C.

D.

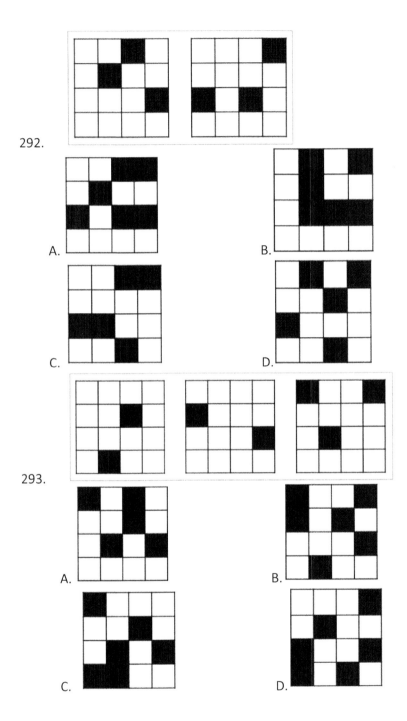

292.

293.

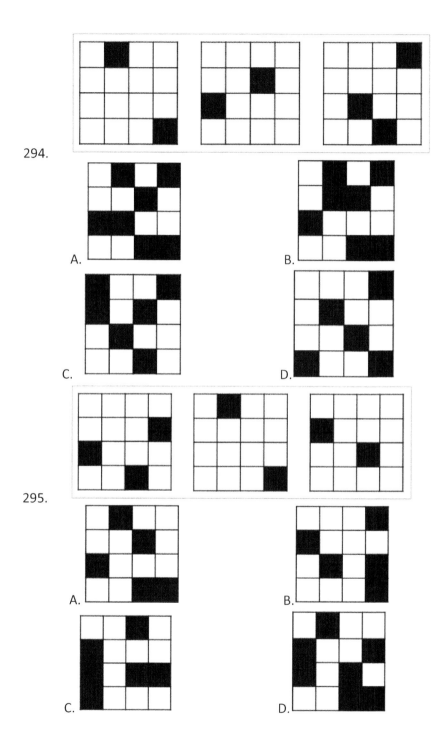

294.

A.

B.

C.

D.

295.

A.

B.

C.

D.

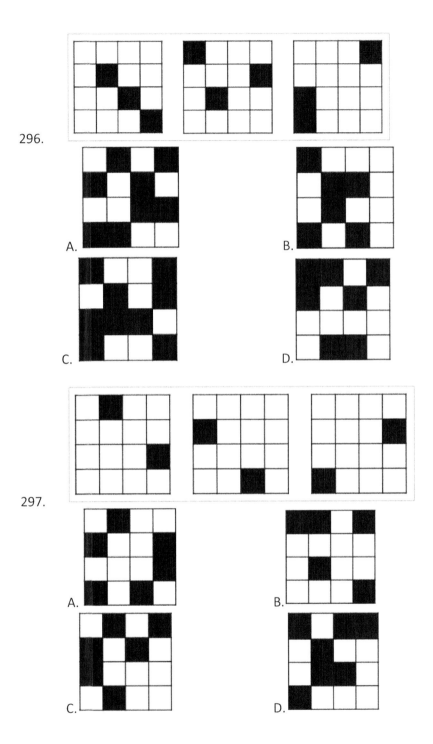

296.

297.

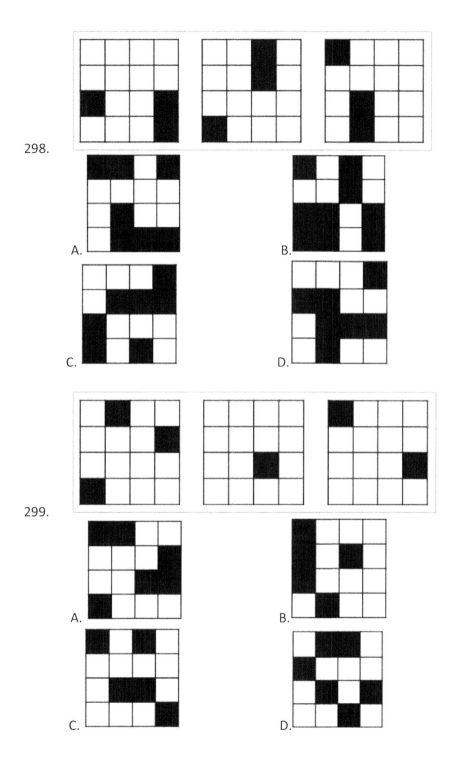

298.

A.

B.

C.

D.

299.

A.

B.

C.

D.

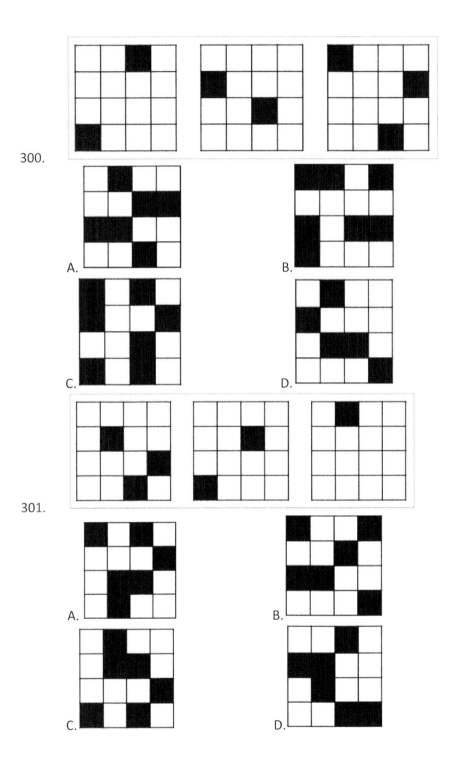

300.

301.

302.

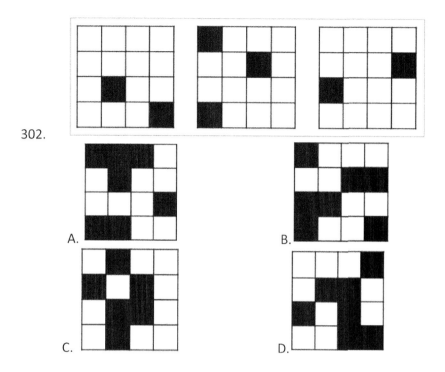

A.

B.

C.

D.

Answer Key

1. B
2. B
3. A
4. C
5. E
6. B
7. C
8. C
9. E

20th Floor - Top Floor
16th Floor – Jonah
14th Floor – Gym
12th Floor – Doug
8th Floor – Sarah
Ashley lives between the 2nd and 8th floor but we don't know precisely
which floor. We know she lives below Sarah, but above Steve since he
is on the bottom floor

2nd Floor - Steve

10. **D**
11. **A**
12. **A**
13. **B**
14. **D**
15. **B**
16. **D**

She started on Friday of week 3. SUVs are produced on Thursday and Adriene did not work on any SUVs.

17. **C**

From largest to smallest
Kory
Amy
Derrick & Lily
Jerome

18. **B**

The smartest dog will be the smallest dog, which is Jerome's

19. **A**
20. **D**

The new order from largest to smallest is now:
Kory
Derrick
Amy& Lily
Jerome

21. **C**
22. **A**

A scratch on the outside of the door is cosmetic damage and therefore Department Q is notified.

23. **E**

An angry customer is a disgruntled customer and therefore the manager should be called.

24. D

25. E

Looking at the far right column, only Management does not receive an incentive for being employee of the Quarter.

26. C

Refer to the third row and fourth column of the table.

27. C

Refer to the third row and third column of the table.

28. D

Refer to the second row and fifth column of the table.

29. B

We know the least number of apples was bought by one of the girls. There are two girls, Abbey and Jill. We know Abbey bought the most apples which leaves only Jill.

30. E

We know Tim bought twice as many apples as Kiley. Among only the boys (Tim, Kiley, Farid) that Farid did not buy the most or least among the three. This means Tim bought the most apples among the boys. We know Jill bought the least number of apples from question 29 and that Abbey did not buy as many as Tim. Therefore, Tim bought the most.

31. A

From most to least number of apples bought
Tim
Abbey
Farid
Kiley
Jill

32. C

We know Tim bought twice as many apples as Kiley and that among just the boys (Tim, Kiley, Farid) that Farid did not buy the most or least among those three. Therefore, Kiley bought the least number of apples among the boys.

33. B

The below table arranges buildings from tallest to shortest

Continent	Country	City	Building
Asia	UAE	Dubai	Burj Khalifa
North America	United States	New York City	One World Trade Center
Europe	Russia	Saint Petersburg	Lakhta
Australia	Australia	Oceania	Q1
South America	Chile	Santiago	Gran Torre
Africa	South Africa	Johannesburg	Carlton Center

34. A

Refer to the table in answer #33
One World Trade Center and the Burj Khalifa are both taller than the Lakhta, however only One World Trade Center is listed as an option and therefore is the correct answer.

35. D

Refer to the table in answer #33

36. C

Refer to the table in answer #33

37. D
38. A

Dustin, Sam, and Dacks only play together on weekends (Saturday or Sunday) since Sunday is the only weekend listed it is the correct answer.

39. C

Dacks and Sam – Age of the Universe
Dacks and Jin – Tetrix
Jin and Dustin – Air Hockey

Dacks, Sam, Dustin – Football
Dustin and Jin – Aligarh

Stella plays CastleNight, but does not play together with anyone else.

40. E

Sam plays the following games
Age of the Universe – Dacks + Sam play together
Eliquis – Sam plays alone

Since Dacks is playing with Jin that leaves Sam to play Eliquis alone.

41. C
42. B

$$\frac{2}{3} \times \frac{4}{8} = \frac{2(4)}{3(8)} = \frac{8}{24} = \frac{1}{3}$$

43. E
44. A

$$5x - 6 = 3x - 8$$

$$2x = -2$$

$$x = \frac{-2}{2}$$

$$x = -1$$

45. D
46. B

$$9^x = 27^2$$

Is equivalent to

$$3^{2x} = 3^{3(2)}$$

$$3^{2x} = 3^6$$

$$2x = 6$$

$$x = \frac{6}{2}$$

$$x = 3$$

47. D

First, simplify expressions involving powers and roots.
$$18 + 36 \div 9$$
Next, multiple and divide before adding or subtracting.
$$18 + 4 =$$
$$= 22$$

48. C

Rewrite the decimal as a fraction with 1 in the denominator
$$\frac{0.56}{1}$$
Multiply by 100 in order to remove the decimal in the numerator
$$\frac{0.56}{1} \times \frac{100}{100} = \frac{56}{100}$$
Reduce the fraction to simplest form
$$\frac{56}{100} = \frac{14}{25}$$

49. E
50. E

Write an equivalent expression that has the same base
$$2^{x+3} = 2^{2(x-2)}$$
$$x + 3 = 2(x - 2)$$
$$x + 3 = 2x - 4$$
$$7 = x$$

51. A

52. E

$$\frac{1}{4}\left(\frac{5}{5}\right) + \frac{4}{5}\left(\frac{4}{4}\right)$$

$$\frac{5}{20} + \frac{16}{20}$$

$$\frac{5 + 16}{20}$$

$$\frac{21}{20}$$

53. D

$$8x = 5(24)$$
$$8x = 120$$

$$x = \frac{120}{8}$$

$$x = 15$$

54. A

$$\frac{1}{3} \times \frac{3}{4} =$$

$$= \frac{1 \times 3}{3 \times 4}$$

$$= \frac{3}{12}$$

$$= \frac{1}{4}$$

55. E
56. C

57. A

$$12 + 2x + 18 = 10$$
$$2x = -20$$
$$x = -10$$

58. D
59. B
60. E

P	Parentheses
E	Exponent
M	Multiplication
D	Division
A	Addition
S	Subtraction

$$8 + 10 \times 3^3 \div 9$$
$$8 + 10 \times 27 \div 9$$
$$8 + 270 \div 9$$
$$8 + 30$$
$$38$$

61. B

$$-1(4x) = 2(6 - 3x)$$
$$-4x = 12 - 6x$$
$$2x = 12$$
$$x = 6$$

62. A

$$\frac{4}{8} + 4\frac{1}{2} =$$

$$= \frac{1}{2} + 4\frac{1}{2}$$

$$= \frac{1}{2} + \frac{2(4) + 1}{2}$$

$$= \frac{1}{2} + \frac{9}{2}$$

$$= \frac{10}{2}$$

$$= 5$$

63. B
64. A

$$\frac{1}{2} \div \frac{1}{6} =$$

$$= \frac{1}{2} \times \frac{6}{1}$$

$$= \frac{6}{2}$$

$$= 3$$

65. D
66. A
67. E
68. E
69. C
70. B

$$5.4 - 1.1 = 4.3$$

71. D
72. C

$$31 - 19 = 12$$

73. E
74. D

The largest amount of ice cream was consumed in September. Based upon the relationship provided in the prompt, September was therefore the hottest.

75. C
76. C

$$9 - 3 = 6$$

77. A

There were 2 units of hot chocolate consumed in October. We are looking for the month which consumed twice that amount, thus 2(2)=4 but of ice cream. In February 4 units of ice cream were consumed.

78. C
79. A

The dots representing Ireland, Greece, Finland, and Norway are nearly in a vertical line. This indicates their populations are roughly the same. The Netherlands lies outside that vertical line.

80. E

The dot for Luxembourg is the largest and therefore has the largest GDP.

81. B

Spain has an area of 500,000 sq km. We are looking for a country that has approximately 250,000 sq km. This corresponds to the United Kingdom.

82. B
83. B

$$90,000 - 50,000 = 40,000$$

84. D

The steepest negative slope represents the largest decline in revenue. This occurs between May and June. Therefore, June reported the largest drop in revenue from the previous month.

85. C
86. C

Train 313 leaves Alexandria at 6:23 p.m. and arrives in Brooke at 7:19 p.m. The train number also has a B which means it allows full-sized bicycles.

87. B

The following trains stop at Rippon:
$301 - 303 - 305 - 307 - 309 - 311 - 313 - 315$

88. A

Dan will arrive in Brooke at 4:36 p.m. while Sarah will arrive at 5:36 p.m. Dan therefore will be waiting 1hr, or 60 minutes.

89. E

Item	Current Inventory	Price for 1	Price when buying 3 or more
Apples	5	£ 1.25	£ 1.20
Oranges	4	£ 0.80	£ 0.75
Grapes	6	£ 5.50	£ 5.25
Lemons	12	£ 0.50	£ 0.40
Pears	8	£ 1.50	£ 1.25
Bananas	2	£ 0.25	£ 0.20

90. E

Customers receive a discounted price when purchasing 3 or more of an item. Since there are only 2 Bananas in inventory it is not possible to receive the discount for 3 or more.

91. C

$$2(5.50) + 3(1.25) + 1.25 + 3(0.75) =$$
$$11 + 3.75 + 1.25 + 2.25 =$$
$$= 18.25$$

92. B

$$26 - [3(0.75) + 0.25 + 2(5.5)] =$$
$$26 - [2.25 + 0.25 + 11] =$$
$$26 - 13.5 =$$
$$= 12.5$$

93. E

The new price for 1x orange would be 0.60. 2x Oranges would therefore be

$$0.6(2) = 1.20$$

94. D

$$5 + 4 + 6 + 12 + 8 + 2 = 37$$

95. A

A single bag of cherries is £ 2.75. Three or more cherries is thus 2.75-0.25= £ 2.50

96. A
97. C
98. D
99. B
100. C
101. A
102. B
103. E
104. B

105.	A
106.	D
107.	E
108.	A
109.	C
110.	B
111.	E
112.	D
113.	A
114.	B
115.	C
116.	E
117.	A
118.	C
119.	B
120.	D
121.	E
122.	B
123.	A
124.	C
125.	E
126.	B
127.	D
128.	E
129.	B
130.	A
131.	C
132.	E
133.	A
134.	D
135.	C
136.	B

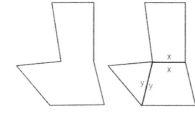

137. E

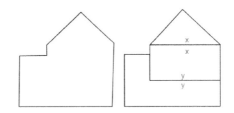

138. A

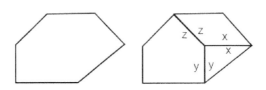

139. D

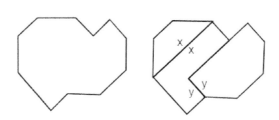

140. B

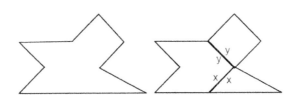

141. E

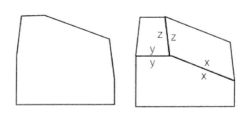

142. C

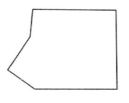 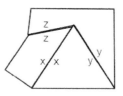

143. A

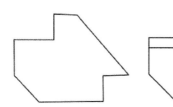

144. D

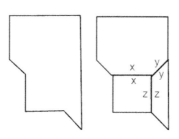

145. A

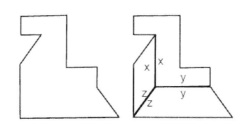

146. E

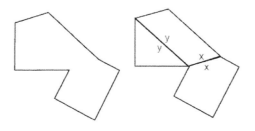

147. B

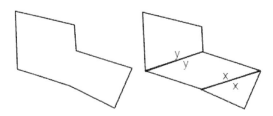

148. A

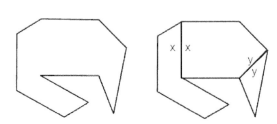

149. D

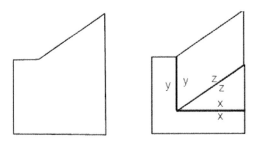

150. B

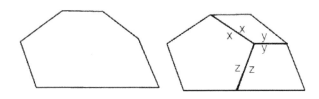

151. C

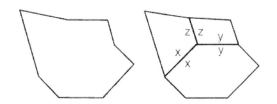

152. E

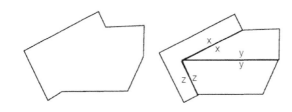

153. D

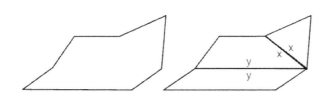

154. B

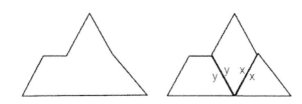

155. A

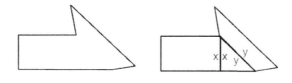

156. C

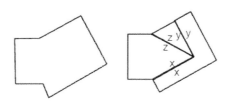

157. C
158. D
159. B
160. D
161. A

162. E
163. C
164. A
165. B
166. D
167. D
168. A
169. E
170. C
171. B
172. E
173. A
174. E
175. D
176. E
177. A
178. D
179. B

The diagram shows the two 3V batteries in parallel. When batteries are in parallel the amp-hours add, but voltage remains constant.

180. A

Energy is equal to power multiplied by time. Kilowatt (KW) is a unit of power and hour (h) is a unit of time.

181. E
182. B

$$R = \frac{V}{I} = \frac{12}{4} = 3\Omega$$

183. A

The resistors are in parallel. The equivalent resistance can be found using:

$$\begin{aligned}
\frac{1}{R_{eq}} &= \frac{1}{R_1} + \frac{1}{R_2} + \frac{1}{R_3} \\
&= \frac{1}{6} + \frac{1}{3} + \frac{1}{2} \\
&= \frac{1}{6} + \frac{1}{3}\left(\frac{2}{2}\right) + \frac{1}{2}\left(\frac{3}{3}\right) \\
&= \frac{1}{6} + \frac{2}{6} + \frac{3}{6} \\
&= \frac{1+2+3}{6} \\
&= \frac{6}{6} \\
&= 1\Omega
\end{aligned}$$

184. C

The resistors are in series. The equivalent resistance can be found from:

$$\begin{aligned}
R_{eq} &= R_1 + R_2 + R_3 + R_4 \\
&= 320 + 320 + 320 + 320 \\
&= 1280\Omega
\end{aligned}$$

185. D

$$2V = I\,\frac{R}{2}$$
$$4V = IR$$
$$4\left(\frac{V}{R}\right) = I$$

186. C

$$I_{Total} = I_1 + I_2$$
$$I = IR + IC$$
$$15 = IR + 4$$

$$IR = 15 - 4$$
$$IR = 11A$$

187. B
188. D
189. E

Find the equivalent resistance for the resistors in parallel
$$\frac{1}{R_{eq}} = \frac{1}{R_1} + \frac{1}{R_2}$$
$$= \frac{1}{1} + \frac{1}{1}$$
$$= \frac{1}{2}$$
$$R_{eq} = 2$$
Sum the resistors in series
$$R = 2 + 4 + 2 = 8\Omega$$

190. A
191. E
192. B
193. E

The largest drop in voltage occurs with the largest resistor
$$V = I \times R$$

194. C
195. B

A resistor reduces both voltage and current, only current is an option.

196. C

$$\text{Current} = \frac{\text{Charge}}{\text{Time}} = \frac{10}{2} = 5A$$

197. B

Electricity is produced when electrons flow from the anode to the cathode. The anode is negatively charged. Electrons are repelled from the anode to the positive cathode.

198. D

The circuit shows three resistors in series with their corresponding voltage drop. The supply voltage is thus:
$$3 + 9 + 8 = 20V$$

199. A

200. E

$$P = I^2 R = 2^2(3) = 4(3) = 12W$$

201. C

202. A

Bulb 1 is in series; when it goes out, it will create an open circuit that will prevent the other bulbs from lighting up.

203. D

204. B

205. E

206. A

207. D

Since the resistors are in parallel the voltage is the same across the branches. Since we are given the current and resistance for the upper branch we can find the voltage:
$$V = IR = 2(6) = 12V$$
The lower branch must also be 12V. Therefore the current for the lower branch is
$$I = \frac{V}{R} = \frac{12}{3} = 4A$$
We know the current must sum across the branches, therefore the ammeter reads
$$2 + 4 = 6A$$

208. C

Since all bulbs go out, it indicates an open circuit which means the bulbs are wired in series.

209. B

210. D

$$2V = I\frac{R}{2}$$

$$4V = IR$$

$$4\left(\frac{V}{R}\right) = I$$

211. A

Since the resistors are in series the equivalent resistance is

$$R_{eq} = 3 + 9 = 12\Omega$$

We can find the current from:

$$I = \frac{V}{R} = \frac{12}{12} = 1A$$

212. E

$$V = IR = 2I(4R) = 8(IR)$$

213. C

214. B

215. D

$$V = V_t\left(\frac{R}{R_1 + R_2}\right)$$

$$= 12\left(\frac{10}{10 + 5}\right)$$

$$= 12\left(\frac{10}{15}\right)$$

$$= 8V$$

216. A

217. D

218. E

$$\frac{3A}{1}\left(\frac{1000mA}{1A}\right) = 3000mA$$

219. C

220.	B
221.	A
222.	A
223.	D

$$W = \text{Force} \times \text{Distance}$$

224.	B
225.	C
226.	C

Calculate the amount of force the 100kg weight is applying. For simplicity let g=10 m/s²

$$F = mg = 100(10) = 1000N$$

Two segments of the rope are pulling on the 100kg block. The minimum amount of force required to lift the block is

$$\frac{1000}{2} = 500N$$

| 227. | E |

$$MA = \frac{D_{wheel}}{D_{axle}} = \frac{64}{8} = 8$$

| 228. | A |

$$\tau = D \times F$$

| 229. | D |

$$\frac{24}{8} \times 12 = 36$$

| 230. | B |

| 231. | B |

$$KE = \frac{1}{2} mv^2$$
$$125 = \frac{1}{2} 10v^2$$
$$125 = 5v^2$$
$$25 = v^2$$
$$v = 5m/s^2$$

232. C

For simplicity let g= 10 m/s²

$$PE = KE$$
$$mgh = \frac{1}{2} mv^2$$
$$gh = \frac{1}{2} v^2$$

Now solve for velocity

$$10(5) = \frac{1}{2} v^2$$
$$50 = \frac{1}{2} v^2$$
$$100 = v^2$$
$$v = 10m/s^2$$

233. A

Torque and speed are inversely proportional

234. E

Calculate the volume of the tank.

$$V = lwh = 200(10)(50) = 100,000m^3$$

From the prompt we are given 1 cubic meter of water = 1000kg.
For simplicity let g=10 m/s²

$$F = mg = 100,000(1000)(10) = 1,000,000,000N$$

Calculate the area at the bottom of the tank

$$A = lw = 10(200) = 2000m^2$$

We can now calculate the pressure

$$P = \frac{F}{A} = \frac{1000000000}{2000} = 500,000N/m^2$$

235. D

When the beam is balanced, it will be in a state of equilibrium.

$$15(3) = 5W$$
$$45 = 5W$$
$$W = 9kg$$

236. B

After 1 minute the container is filled with 60 liters of water (120-60=60). In order to reach 220 liters, it will take

$$\frac{210}{60} = 3.5$$

237. A

238. C

239. B

240. B

Identical springs arranged in parallel will compress half the distance of the same springs arranged in series.

$$\frac{8}{2} = 4cm$$

241. D

The ratio of diameters of wheel M compared to wheel Y is 2:1. Every revolution wheel M makes, wheel Y & N (since Y and N are connected) will be 2x revolutions. Likewise, the ratio of wheel N to wheel Z is also 2:1. Since wheel N makes 2x revolutions that means wheel Z will make 4x revolutions 2(2)=4

242. C

For simplicity let g=10 m/s²

$$PE = KE$$
$$mgh = \frac{1}{2}mv^2$$
$$gh = \frac{1}{2}v^2$$
$$10(20) = \frac{1}{2}v^2$$
$$v^2 = 400$$
$$v = 20m/s$$

243. C

Hooke's law states

$$F = kx$$

This is a proportional relationship. Since the mass of the object increases by 1/2, the force will also increase by 1/2 which means the springs length will increase by ½ as well.

$$6 + 6\left(\frac{1}{2}\right) = 9\text{cm}$$

244.   E

$$140 \times (1 - 0.85) = 21\text{hp}$$

245.   C

$$a = \frac{\Delta v}{\Delta t} = \frac{45 - 15}{2} = 15m/s^2$$

246.   A

Vectors have both magnitude and direction.

247.   B

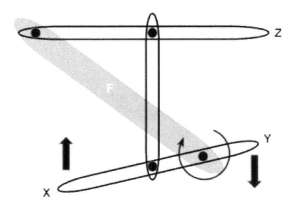

248.   C
249.   E
250.   D

In an elastic collision, the total kinetic energy remains the same. Since the bowling ball did not move, the other ball must maintain its current level of kinetic energy. Because the bowling ball didn't move after the collision it means small ball will move to the left afterward.

251.   B
252.   C

$$m_1 v_1 + m_2 v_2 = (m_1 + m_2) v_f$$
$$24000(8) + 8000(0) = (24000 + 8000) v_f$$
$$192000 + 0 = 32000 v_f$$
$$v_f = 6m/s$$

253. E

Since all gears are identical, they will all turn at 12 rpm.

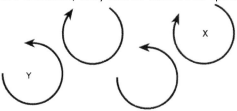

254. D

$$F = kx$$
$$600 = k\left(\frac{10}{100}\right)$$
$$600 = k0.1$$
$$k = 6000N/m$$

255. A

Calculate the area of the pedestal.
$$A = lw = 3(5) = 15m^2$$
The pressure can be calculated from
$$P = \frac{F}{A} = \frac{1500}{15} = 100\text{Pa}$$

256. C

The pressure at B will be greater than A since Gage B is located below the vessel.

257. B

$$W = Fd = 9(18) = 162\text{ J}$$

258. E

A vector has both magnitude and direction

259. D

$$P = \frac{F}{A} = \frac{2F}{2A} = \frac{F}{A}$$

260. A

A rise in atmospheric pressure causes the fluid in the tube to rise.

261. A

Since gear 1 is turning clockwise, it means gear 2 is turning counter clockwise.

$$\frac{speed_1}{speed_2} = \frac{teeth_2}{teeth_1}$$

$$\frac{40}{speed_2} = \frac{80}{20}$$

$$speed_2 = 10 \, \text{rpm}$$

262.	B
263.	A
264.	C
265.	C
266.	D
267.	B
268.	A
269.	A
270.	C
271.	B
272.	D
273.	A
274.	B
275.	C
276.	D
277.	A
278.	A
279.	C
280.	C
281.	B
282.	D
283.	C
284.	A
285.	D
286.	D
287.	A
288.	D
289.	C
290.	B

291.	D
292.	A
293.	B
294.	A
295.	D
296.	C
297.	A
298.	B
299.	A
300.	C
301.	C
302.	B

Printed in Great Britain
by Amazon